INTERNAL
POWER

INTERNAL POWER

(7)

DOORWAYS

TO SELF DISCOVERY

HAROLD W. BECKER

NEW WORLD LIBRARY
SAN RAFAEL, CALIFORNIA

Published by New World Library
58 Paul Drive
San Rafael, CA 94903

Cover Design: Kathy Warinner
Text Design & Typography: Becky Benenate

Library of Congress Cataloging-in-Publication Data
Becker, Harold W., 1962 —
    Internal power : seven doorways to self-discovery / Harold
W. Becker.
      p. cm.
    ISBN 1-880032-31-7 (alk. paper) : $11.95
    1. Self-actualization (Psychology) 2. Self-perception. I. Title.
BF637.S4B43   1993   93-19843
158'.1—dc20   CIP

ISBN: 1-880032-31-7
First Printing: October, 1993
Printed in the U.S.A. on acid-free paper
Distibuted by Publishers Group West

10 9 8 7 6 5 4 3 2 1

This book is dedicated to you, the reader.
As we travel together on this journey called
Life, may we touch one another with our love
and become that which we really are.

Acknowledgments

I have been richly blessed with the opportunity to share my life with many special people. Each one has guided and supported my efforts, and each has been a beacon of love to keep me on course through the dark and foggy passages.

To my father, Horst Becker — without your wisdom, courage, and special love and support, this book may never have made its way. You set the example; I merely followed.

To my mother, Gisela Becker — you have held me in your heart and have nurtured my unlimited potential. Your unquenchable thirst for knowledge rubs off on me in many wonderful ways.

To my friend, John Goltz — you have stood by me for several years and have made sure I stayed on track. Your unconditional love, dedication, and sincere application of the work I do has made it all worthwhile.

To the staff of New World Library — you have recognized the merit of this work and have believed in me enough to publish this book. I greatly appreciate your loving efforts.

Finally, to every person I have met and shared with along the way — you have supported me in ways you will never know. Those smiles and hugs energized every word in this book. Thank you all.

Table of Contents

A Letter to My Readers   xii
Introduction   1

    THE SEVEN DOORWAYS: AN OVERVIEW   5

The Seven Doorways   6
The Grand Hallway   8
The Golden Key   8
Visualizations   9
Playtime   10
Some Additional Thoughts   11

    THE GRAND HALLWAY   13

A Visualization   13

    DOORWAY ONE: CHOICE   17

A Visualization   17
Choice   18
Summary   34
Playtime   35

DOORWAY TWO: COMMUNICATION 37

A Visualization 37
Communication 38
Four Methods of Communication 44
Summary 53
Playtime 55

DOORWAY THREE: POSITIVE THINKING 57

A Visualization 57
Positive Thinking 58
Affirmations 69
Summary 75
Playtime 76

DOORWAY FOUR: CREATIVITY 79

A Visualization 79
Creativity 80
Summary 91
Playtime 93

DOORWAY FIVE:
MASCULINE AND FEMININE ENERGIES 95

A Visualization 95
Masculine and Feminine Energies 96
Summary 108
Playtime 110

DOORWAY SIX: THE CHILD WITHIN   113

A Visualization   113
The Child Within   114
Summary   133
Playtime   134

DOORWAY SEVEN:
UNCONDITIONAL LOVE   135

A Visualization   135
Unconditional Love   137
Summary   159
Playtime   162

A NEW BEGINNING   165

Being Ourselves   168
The Journey Continues   175

EPILOGUE   177

A Letter to My Readers

Several years ago I found myself at a crossroad in life. I had been at this juncture before, yet this time it was different because I intuitively knew I would make a crucial decision about my life. I needed to know who I really was, and the inner urge to explore myself led me to begin a journey of discovery. The book you are about to read is a culmination of the experience and understanding that came from the decision I made.

Before I started my journey of self-discovery, I was like most people I knew. I thought I existed to fulfill a destiny that others dictated to me. I began to realize that there had to be more to life than I was experiencing, but my structured ways were keeping me from it. Relationships and friendships were generally struggles — and material things brought only momentary joy.

On the surface I was a respected manager with a graduate degree in business. I had many friends and had traveled extensively. I appeared confident, balanced, motivated, and successful. Yet these appearances often masked my unhappiness and depression, anxiety and fear.

As I began to notice the connection between my thoughts and the reality I experienced, an inner urge began to motivate me. I needed to know more about this connection. I decided to leave my "secure" life and pursue a path of self-discovery. Even though I had limited finances, I quit my job and left the place I had lived for twenty years. I was convinced of three things: I wanted to help people, I wanted to pursue my dreams, and I knew I was the only one who could make my life work.

Because I had no special training in or understanding of how to help myself, I stumbled and fell many times. With every tumble I became more determined to discover who I really was and to uncover the thoughts I had underneath the surface. I was committed to do whatever work was necessary — my very happiness and peace depended on it. I embarked on a path that would take me to new heights of experience, and I came face to face with some of the lowest aspects of my nature. I gathered every resource and researched every avenue that promised personal growth.

As I explored my thoughts and beliefs, I learned how to release old patterns of thinking that bound me to limitation in life. Eventually I found myself entering each of the Seven Doorways described in this book. Entering each doorway prepared me for the next one. I let go of the need to be "right" for others and learned how to think and be right for myself. Through my process of self-discovery I became aware that I am an unlimited person capable of creating anything I truly desire.

Entering the doorways of discovery has been the most rewarding and enjoyable process I have ever experienced. Naturally, there have been numerous challenging times to endure, but each had its reward in understanding and strength. I learned to make my thoughts work for me, and I have become happy and peaceful within. For the first time in my life I am exactly where I want to be, doing the things I want to do. I create and live my ultimate dreams.

This book is really about all of us and how we can become the unlimited people we really are. Like the many people who have walked before me and have cleared the way to make my personal growth so much easier, I hope that sharing the most powerful and useful aspects of my journey will help you walk more lightly on your path to self discovery. This is my gift of love to you. Thank you for taking this journey with me as we explore our hidden — yet unlimited — potential.

Introduction

Welcome! We will be taking a wonderful journey together as you read this book. I will be your host and guide throughout. Together, you and I will explore seven areas of life that can provide a framework for understanding our inner selves.

The Seven Doorways presented in this book are gateways to the vast potential that exists within each of us. I believe these ideas will have a profound and positive impact on your current reality, and will provide new insights on some old, traditional beliefs. Some special techniques are included to help overcome any personal limitations. By the time we end our journey together, I hope you will have some wonderful and helpful new perspectives on life's unlimited possibilities.

This is a book about life — about who we are, what we think we know and believe, and what we really know. It is about our human potential: a vast, infinite process of learning, understanding, and creating. It is about freedom within; it is a guide to understanding our true selves. There is nothing magical within this book; rather, the magic resides within each of us as *Internal Power*. Uncovering our true selves is a journey, not a goal — it is a fulfilling process we choose to undertake. This book offers many opportunities to expand your awareness and to help you find your Internal Power — your unlimited abilities and talents.

Because this book is about personal freedom, carefully consider what is presented and accept only those parts that feel right to you. Never accept ideas that don't ring true for you, for you alone hold the key to your Internal Power.

THE POWER OF THOUGHT

The most important concept of this book can be summed up in a few words: We are our thoughts. In other words, this marvelous event we call Life is really a series of our thoughts and experiences. Our thoughts constantly shift perspective, depending on what occurs in our lives, and the reality we experience depends on what perspectives we take in our thoughts. Our thoughts are, therefore, the source of our Internal Power. When we recognize, understand, and learn to work with our thoughts, we can embrace life in its fullness, with all its unlimited potential.

Understanding our thoughts and perspectives on life becomes very important when we realize that our thoughts have energy. Our thoughts provide energy to create our physical world. When we use our bodies to create actions or words, we transform the energy from our thoughts into physical actions. This is a simple but powerful acknowledgment. When we have low thoughts that are based in fear or anxiety, we significantly limit our energy. When we engage our higher, unlimited thoughts, however, we energize ourselves to create anything we want. Our thoughts provide the energy of action!

Our thoughts provide the
energy to create our world.

Our Internal Power is generated by using the energy of our thoughts to transform and energize our lives. When we learn to pay attention to our thoughts, alter certain perspectives, and engage the most powerful thoughts we have, we discover our true selves. This internal process will literally create a different reality for us, but it may not happen overnight. It takes an active and persistent commitment on our part to want the best that life has to offer and be willing to pursue it. The key is to be open to change and then to take action.

Whenever we choose to make a change in life, we cannot put it off to some future time, for our future exists only in thought. The way to create our future is to act on the thoughts we have right now, in this moment. The past is also but a thought and need be of no concern to us because we cannot physically change our past — we can only change our thought perspectives about it. If we are ever going to tap our unlimited potential, we must work with the *now moment.*

Pause and think for a moment. What did you do yesterday around noon? Is the activity you are recalling right now physically happening, or is it a thought in the form of a memory? It is a thought, isn't it? What about tomorrow? What will you conceivably be doing around noon? Many possibilities may come to mind, and each scenario represents a thought projected into tomorrow. If yesterday is a thought and tomorrow is a thought, when is the only physical moment we have to act? Right now. Our past is a thought memory and our future is a thought potential, so now is the only moment we have to change our thoughts and, therefore, our reality.

In the present moment, we hold the key to our Internal Power.

The Seven Doorways:
An Overview

We will pass through Seven Doorways on our exciting journey. Each doorway represents an opportunity to unfold the hidden potential within us and to fully realize our Internal Power. Our Internal Power is a magnificent reservoir of energy waiting to be tapped, and the structure and metaphors in this book will assist in discovering and working with this dynamic inner energy source.

The Seven Doorways that lead to self-discovery are Choice, Communication, Positive Thinking, Creativity, Masculine and Feminine Energies, The Child Within, and Unconditional Love. First, we'll look at a brief summary of the doorways; then we'll see how we can enter them.

THE SEVEN DOORWAYS

Doorway One: Choice

The foundation of our journey to self-discovery is *choice*. We must recognize that we are responsible for our lives through the choices we make, which in turn create the lives we live. We must also consider the intent behind our choices. Thus, two important dimensions of choice are responsibility and intent.

Doorway Two: Communication

We obtain and process information through our auditory, visual, and kinesthetic senses, although one form of processing may dominate the others. In addition, there are four methods of communication: internal, external, physical, and nonphysical. By recognizing how we communicate in these areas and by learning to improve our effectiveness, we begin to enhance our Internal Power.

Doorway Three: Positive Thinking

Positive thinking is the road to joy and happiness within. When we begin to understand that a positive perspective leads to a positive reality, we empower our every moment. This thought transformation leads to wonderful levels of calm and peace. By using a variety of techniques, we can quickly put positive thinking to use and immediately benefit from the results. Positive thinking is one of the most powerful methods to personal transformation.

Doorway Four: Creativity

Creativity is the essence of our lives. Everything we do is first created in our minds as thoughts. We then take action, if we so desire, to create the physical equivalents of our thoughts. By definition, then, we are all creative beings. Restoring this understanding into our everyday lives leads to magical results. When we begin to view the power and beauty that resides within our imagination, we can use the power of our imagination to create a most wonderful life.

Doorway Five: Masculine and Feminine Energies

Within each person is a combination of masculine and feminine energies. Knowing that we are creative beings with imagination — a feminine energy — is wonderfully enhanced by our ability to bring about physical reality through willpower — a masculine energy. Regardless of our gender, we can embrace the magnificent harmony of balancing these powerful energies within us. As we recognize that balance comes from using both parts of ourselves, we are better able to transform our imagination into physical reality.

Doorway Six: The Child Within

Embracing the child within leads us to the heart of a wonderful, spontaneous, and incredible friendship — the friendship with our child self. We can bring this vibrant energy back into our lives and begin to explore vast areas of untapped potential. We can give our child within the love, care, and trusting relationship it has always sought, and this bonding friendship not only will last a lifetime, but also will reap great rewards.

Doorway Seven: Unconditional Love

The final doorway is the culmination of our journey of self-discovery. When we embrace unconditional love, we begin to fully radiate the Internal Power that lives within each of us. Setting aside fear, anger, doubt, pain, and suffering, we can allow love to flow freely throughout our lives. Love is all-knowing, calming, and peaceful. Love transcends all darkness and brings beautiful light back into our lives. Our Internal Power is greatest when we realize unconditional love for ourselves and for all things.

THE GRAND HALLWAY

The Seven Doorways are connected by a wonderful Grand Hallway. This hallway is meant to represent our inner selves, a metaphor for our solid inner structure, and each doorway represents a dimension of our inner potential. These doorways to the self are only limited by our imagination and desire. As we move through the hallway and enter each door, we will expand our awareness and understanding, and begin the journey to inner freedom and peace.

THE GOLDEN KEY

The Golden Key allows us to open the seven doors and represents our individual *willingness*. Our Golden Key to

Life was presented to us at birth, and we control its use at all times. No one can ever take it away, and it cannot be lost.

You have complete control to open any door with your key, and you also may leave at any time. You control the movement in and out of the door, and you control the pace of your journey. You may choose to return numerous times to explore what is valuable for you within each doorway.

VISUALIZATIONS

We will use visualizations to enter the Grand Hallway and to open the seven doors. A visualization is an internal contemplation or meditation in which you learn to quiet your mind and focus your thoughts on a particular image. This mental picture is created by your thoughts and imagination at work.

The visualizations in this book set the stage for the material you will be reading. Details are purposefully left out so you can create mental images that are meaningful to you. The Grand Hallway, for example, can be used as a safe place, but your own visualization may be used to make you feel safe. You can create a mental image of a location — a beach, the woods, a garden — and choose to make this spot free from outside influence. You can then go to this retreat in your thoughts for a quiet moment or time out whenever you like. You control your thoughts, and you control your visualization.

If you are not familiar with the technique of visualization, here is a brief explanation:

(1) To effectively do a visualization, you must have a few minutes without interruption so you can focus on the visualization without becoming distracted. After you know you have a few moments and a quiet place, you can begin to relax.

(2) To start, take some deep breaths and begin to clear your mind of worry, frustration, or other random thoughts. Calming yourself down is an important part of the visualization process. Allow random thoughts to pass by without dwelling on them.

(3) When you feel peaceful and relaxed, open this book to one of the visualizations that begins each chapter. Allow yourself time to experience the mental picture, to experience the details of each door and room. You deserve this opportunity and it is time well spent.

(4) When you finish your visualization, bring yourself back into the room where you are sitting and become aware of your physical surroundings. Then begin to read the chapter that follows the visualization.

PLAYTIME

At the end of each chapter is a section called "Playtime." Playtime is an opportunity for you to integrate the ideas and experience the material you have just read. You will find these activities light and fun, and they will help you to experience the concepts firsthand. You can do them as often as you wish; each encounter will bring about a new experience. You may also choose to develop your own variations.

SOME ADDITIONAL THOUGHTS

As you read this material, establish the pace that is right for you. Allow yourself time to assimilate the ideas as you proceed through each doorway. This book is intended to be a guide or manual that gently stimulates you into new awareness every time you pick it up. Often, reading a section over again at a later date will bring new meaning or insight, especially as your awareness broadens.

If you have the opportunity to share this journey with another person — a friend, loved one, spouse, companion — please do! The journey of self-discovery is far more exciting, enjoyable, and satisfying when we do it together, when we know we are loved and supported by a fellow traveler. Both people must, however, share in the desire to grow and become unlimited through the Internal Power process. Never attempt to force another person; it will not work in the long run.

Enjoy your journey through the Seven Doorways. Acknowledging your Internal Power is a wonderful experience — one that you will find everlasting. I hope you enjoy this guide as much as I enjoyed creating it for you.

The Grand Hallway

A VISUALIZATION

As we begin our journey, we find ourselves standing at the entrance of a long, elaborate hallway. The walls ascend majestically until they connect with the ceiling high above. A splendid light permeates every corner of the elongated room — there are no shadows, just beautiful illumination. We can see everything clearly, even at the far end of this magnificent corridor.

We cast our eyes upon the walls. They radiate our favorite color, which emanates with such a luster that we feel it beckoning us to touch and experience the color itself. We feel a warm, glowing feeling as we gaze upon this room, and we are invited to explore its every possibility. As we look at the sides of the hallway, we notice the intricate detail and splendor before us. The walls have an ornate molding that is at once complex yet simple.

The elegant floor is covered by a lush, deep carpet of the most delicate hue. It blends and combines the seven colors of the rainbow into a translucent cloud that appears to almost suspend the hallway, yet it provides a solid foundation for our journey.

We look up the walls to the ceiling, stopping only momentarily to take in the splendor of the design. The walls fold delicately into the domed ceiling, forming a union of strength and bonding that keeps the structure solid. The ceiling has its own illumination, beaming the light that saturates the entire hallway and drawing all the parts together into one complete whole.

We shift our gaze back to the walls and notice seven distinct doorways. Three are on the right, three are on the left, and a double set of doors graces the far end of the Grand Hallway, directly opposite where we stand. Each door is embellished with its distinct, decorated entryway. Our imagination fills with ideas while our curiosity about what lies behind each door grows. We stand with increasing excitement and anticipation, waiting to explore each gateway before us. We know our entry is secured by the Golden Key we hold — the key of *willingness.*

The private space of our hallway has an energy and life of its own. We hear wonderful, uplifting tones of music, and our hearts expand as we realize that this beautiful hallway is ours to use and enjoy always. No one can enter unless we invite them in. We can add our most prized and favorite possessions at any time to further decorate the hallway; we can bring the beauty of ourselves into this place and feel peace within.

We are now ready to move along our journey, which will bring us peace, love, and healing if we allow them to come. We will put the Golden Key of Life to use — our willingness to find the love that resides within us. Through all we encounter, love lights our way and penetrates our fears so that they dissolve instantly. With this faith in ourselves, we move to the first of the Seven Doorways.

Doorway One:
Choice

A VISUALIZATION

We step softly, our Golden Key in hand, toward the first door. Our feet seem to glide across the plush carpet, as if we are gently carried to the door. Our anticipation grows. We look at the doorway that stands before us and admire its design.

The door is of a solid, burnished wood, with a deep luster and polished look. It is intricately designed, with etched surfaces. There is a golden slotted plate for our key; in the center of the door is a solid gold doorknob. We quickly place our key in the slot and turn the key. The door opens slowly.

We linger at our first doorway for only a moment and then proceed into a room brightly lit with hundreds of twinkling lights. The colors dance and sparkle around us as if we had wandered into the middle of a kaleidoscope.

As we step farther in, we become surrounded by these lights. A warm, cozy feeling comes over us. It occurs to us that we have entered the room of our thoughts, our thinking mind.

At first we hesitate, wondering if the lights are disorienting us in some way, but we realize that the myriad of lights are quite soothing. They are friendly and inviting, for they are our very thoughts.

When we focus more clearly, we notice that the hundreds of lights cluster so they form letters and words. We then see that the letters and words are messages to help us create what we want in our lives. As we look clearly at each cluster of lights and concentrate on it, we understand the meaning of each message. The individual lights become the actual thoughts in our mind.

CHOICE

This incredible journey we call *Life* is paved by the choices we make along the way. Every moment of every day, we can choose a new path, a new beginning, a new reality — and a new way of life. We have the unlimited potential within to be everything we ever dreamed of being and more, much more.

The process of self-discovery begins with the choices we make. This is the cornerstone, the foundation of our journey through the Seven Doorways to Internal Power. We possess the ability to choose and act upon the thoughts we have, allowing us to create the reality we want. What a powerful opportunity!

What are choices? They are the decisions we make from moment to moment, the kinds of thoughts we choose to entertain. Everything we experience in life comes from our thoughts. If we want to manifest something physically in our lives, we first think about it, and then make numerous decisions until we accomplish our goal.

Think for a moment about the many decisions that occur, for example, when you go for a loaf of bread at the supermarket. If the thought of buying bread occurs to you at home, you do what is necessary to prepare yourself to get in the car, drive to the store, and make your purchase. Although most of your physical effort is spent just obtaining the bread, your thoughts continue at an incredible pace — thoughts of finances, experiences, desires, fantasies, emotions, and so on run through your mind.

In our simple example, we have not considered the other interactions or distractions that normally occur while going to the supermarket. Such situations multiply our thoughts many times over.

Even when we are physically quiet, our thoughts never cease. What do we do during "quiet time"? We may read, watch a sunset, listen to music, daydream, meditate, contemplate, pray, take a bath, go biking or jogging. What are we also doing during this time? Thinking, of course! The process never ceases. Even when we sleep, our mind continues to think as we dream. And with every thought, we have an opportunity for choice. We have the chance to accept or reject any thought and to alter it or change it to a new one.

Without our thoughts, we would cease to exist; we must think in order to function in life. We can observe and experience our physical world only through the thoughts we have in our minds. Without thought, what would there be?

Conscious and Unconscious Thought

We choose the lives we lead through a combination of conscious and unconscious thought. For too many of us, the unconscious thought process is permitted to dominate our thinking and govern the majority of choices in our lives. We surrender our conscious choice to this unconscious process. The first doorway delivers conscious choice back into our thinking, allowing us to bring our unlimited potential into focus.

Unconscious thought is being unaware of our thoughts. It is what most of us engage in throughout most of our days, because we lack the training to pay attention to what we think. When we don't pay attention to the thoughts we have, we allow memories, experiences, fears, guilt, emotions, and other people's beliefs to run our lives. We give our Internal Power to others, to society, to the moment, to an event. We allow the thought processes of others to control our thinking instead of following our inner truth and guidance.

Unconscious thought is a process in which we allow our habitual thought patterns and emotions to over-influence or intensify an experience and, therefore, lead us astray. In this reactive state, we often receive a flood of disturbing thoughts and limited perspectives that combine with a general fear of the future. When we are unconscious, or not in control of our thoughts, we often do and say things that we wouldn't do or say otherwise.

You *can* choose your thoughts and decide what is right for you. There's no need to give your power away to an unconscious process or to accept the views and perspectives of others. Unlimited potential becomes a reality when you learn how to think in unlimited ways, choosing the highest and best thoughts that are appropriate. You can, of course, continue to think unconsciously and in limiting ways. The choice is yours.

We can become fully aware of our thoughts — and aware of the power they have — and begin to use their unlimited potential to our advantage. At the moment we begin to actively work with our thoughts, we bring conscious choice into our lives, which is the key to our unlimited potential. When we learn how to shift our thinking process from unconscious thought to conscious thought, our choices begin to reflect our dreams and desires, and we begin to live those dreams.

You can transform your life by simply paying attention to what you think! The concept of conscious thought puts you back in touch with *your* thoughts. When you begin to acknowledge the kinds of thoughts you have, the focus and power they have in your life, and the choices you are making with them, you can learn to redirect thoughts that are not in alignment with your highest and greatest good. You can literally adjust your thoughts in a positive, conscious way.

And when you develop your ability to take control of random thoughts, you'll discover that your Internal Power is truly unlimited.

What are we really doing when we engage conscious thought? We are paying attention, aware at any moment whether or not our thoughts are congruent with our beliefs and goals. Conscious thinking allows us to have conscious choice. When a thought or thought process is different than we wish it to be, we can invoke our conscious choice to change its focus. Conscious thought means being aware of ourselves as individuals and acting on what we know.

Conscious thinking allows us
to have conscious choice.

When we shift from unconscious thought to conscious thought, we regain control over our thoughts. Random thoughts no longer guide and dictate our perspectives. As we alter our perspectives to include a higher and greater awareness, an acceptance of self and others, and a more loving approach to life, we experience a change in our mental and physical worlds.

Some may ask, "Aren't we always engaged in the process of conscious thought?" Not usually. In our rapidly changing world, information and technology have outpaced our ability to use them. We are bombarded by change from every direction, so we create structure, routine, and habits for our daily activities to avoid the need to consciously think about certain situations and to slow the pace a bit. But when we engage in our routines, fresh ideas and experiences don't come as easily; our routines and habits become forms of escape. We can reverse this process by learning to shift our thinking back to conscious thought and bring choice back into our lives.

Why are conscious thought and choice so important? Because our thoughts have energy; they motivate us to take action in life. Through our thoughts we pursue education, jobs, families, friends, and material possessions. Through our thoughts we pursue peace, acceptance, wisdom, fulfillment, and love; through them we use our imagination and creativity. When you consciously align your thoughts with your highest dreams and desires, you unleash your Internal Power. You become energized by your thoughts, and your thoughts become powerful allies.

Positive and Negative Thought

To further our understanding, let's discuss two broad categories of thought: positive and negative. Positive thoughts empower life and provide unlimited energy whenever we use them. They encourage acceptance toward ourselves and others, and include thoughts of love, peace, harmony, beauty, and happiness. Positive thoughts are thoughts of unlimited potential and are the source of abundant life, encouraging us to become more aware, respectful, kind, compassionate, charitable, and grateful. Positive thoughts enable us to see life as a giant learning process. They help us know that we can conquer any problem before us.

Positive thoughts are thoughts
of unlimited potential.

Negative thoughts are characterized by feelings of fear, guilt, hatred, spite, anger, and frustration. They are kindled by feelings like worry, anxiety, manipulation, bigotry, discrimination, and judgment. Negative thoughts include all forms of limiting beliefs; when we allow them to become an active part of our lives, we exhibit our limited beliefs about ourselves.

Negative thoughts come from a variety of sources. We often accept the negative beliefs of others, allowing their teachings and experiences to become our perspectives without giving ourselves a chance to choose our own views.

One of the greatest sources of negative thoughts is fear. Fear has its uses in certain situations, but it shouldn't immobilize us in daily life. Fear is the ultimate limiting belief. Whether it is fear of death, fear of being alone, fear of failure, fear of success, fear of embarrassment, or fear of the future, this negative thought form is rooted in the belief that we cannot overcome a particular situation. Learning to recognize fearful thoughts within ourselves will greatly assist us in our process of overcoming negative thoughts.

Another source of negative thought comes from our experiences. We use the past as a template — a gauge or pattern — to direct us through current situations. This works well when our experiences have been successful. However, when we make mistakes and don't acknowledge them as a part of the learning process, we may feel angry or guilty. Many of our past experiences didn't work out as we had hoped or expected, and if we bring that negative energy into our current situation, we are bound to create failure once again.

Negative thought keeps us in a confined loop or cycle. We become drawn into a spiral similar to a tornado or whirlpool, and as it grows other negative thoughts are dragged in.

Negative thoughts are not always wrong or bad thoughts — rather, they often point the way to higher thinking if we allow them to. When we choose to acknowledge a negative thought we can then immediately replace it with a more positive thought. If left unchecked, however, the energy of negative thought can become debilitating and can drain the life force out of us.

When we continue to use negative thoughts, we perpetuate the belief that we are limited and powerless. This conflicts with our higher intuitive knowing that recognizes our unlimited nature. To restore the balance in our lives, we can consciously choose positive thoughts and an unlimited perspective.

Positive thoughts expand our awareness, linking together like a chain, creating the things we want in life. Positive thoughts provide the energy to overcome any difficulty. We believe in ourselves, know our abilities, and bring joy and happiness to ourselves and others.

Understanding Choice

To fully incorporate the principle of choice, let's see how it applies in our lives. One of the most difficult interactions we can have is an argument with a friend or loved one.

By their design, arguments are never win-win propositions. Let's see why.

When we begin to argue, we rely on our thoughts to defend and protect us and expound "our points of view." Fueled by individual thoughts and negative and reactionary emotional clusters of thought, our past experiences and fears are brought to the forefront. We may quickly grab these thoughts and act upon them by yelling or physically pounding our fists on tables. The argument feeds on constant streams of thoughts that flood our minds. Every statement we angrily say is returned by a similar statement from the other person. This retaliation makes us even more defensive and reactive. Our mental tornado begins to take shape, hooking any negative thought within its path. The power of spontaneous and unconscious negative thought has been unleashed.

As emotions and feelings begin to surface, clusters of negative thought become more random and more defensive. Our egos are attempting to protect themselves at any cost, and we say and do many things we would never dream of saying or doing under normal circumstances. Our thoughts are attempting to defend our positions and protect us from defeat. Ironically, defeat is all that can come out of arguments.

Through the use of unconscious thought we have given our Internal Power to the argument. We have forgotten all about choice. The only choice we have made is to involve ourselves in a limiting event: the argument. Who can benefit from this kind of situation?

What would happen if we were to stop the moment we

realize an argument was about to begin and carefully observe ourselves and listen to the other person as well? What do we see, and what do we feel? The moment we stop to reflect, we engage our Internal Power. We begin to pay attention to the situation — and, more important, to our thoughts. This conscious process gives us the opportunity to invoke choice, which leads to the appropriate thoughts necessary to remedy the situation.

Because arguments always rage *in our minds* as negative thought conflicts, when we allow our positive thoughts to surface we usually find solutions. When we engage our thoughts in a conscious way, we recognize a potential argument for what it truly is: a disagreement of thought between two parties. Arguments are always about differences of opinion and perspective. Problems, on the other hand — the focus of an argument — can be solved by discussion, by finding mutual agreement and solution. An argument only accentuates the differences in points of view; a solution occurs when we agree on fundamentals and allow ourselves to resolve the situation. Solutions involve cooperation rather than confrontation.

When you are proactive — instead of reactive — you literally diffuse the other person's negative thoughts along with yours, dissolving the potential for an argument. When you choose positive thought over negative thought, the other person has no one to argue with.

It takes practice to engage conscious choice, but the results for everyone involved are definitely worth the practice. The next time you think an argument is beginning, *stop and reflect.* Pause for a moment and pay attention to your thoughts. Acknowledge and release any negative thought or emotion, and choose the conscious, positive thoughts that will show you how to find an appropriate solution.

Freedom and Choice

Choice. Isn't that our ultimate freedom? As human beings we have the freedom of thought. We can choose the kinds of thoughts we have, the perspectives and beliefs we want, and the types of reality we wish to experience. Even in the most distressing situations, we possess the ability to view the event in many ways, from awful to joyful.

Many of us give our choices freely to people and events in our lives, allowing others to control us by accepting their beliefs and perspectives. We allow circumstances and events to overshadow our desires and wishes. We let our past experiences dictate our current reality by accepting the limiting beliefs and prior mistakes as the "way it will always be." We also give our choice to our negative thoughts, such as fear.

What goes on in our thoughts also goes on in our lives. For example, if we feel anger and hurt within, we generally experience angry and hurtful events externally. If we choose to begin the process of redirecting our thoughts in more positive ways, then a corresponding shift will begin to occur in our experiences as well. If we smile, we receive smiles back. If we yell, people often yell back. *Smiling and yelling both start as thoughts in the mind.*

As we consciously pay attention to our thoughts, we create new opportunities for personal growth. When we are not conscious of our thoughts, we stagnate and repeat the same actions to the point of dull routine. Then growth and awareness cease. Life becomes a struggle instead of a joyful opportunity. The reverse is also true: Through conscious thought, we create happy, inspired, beautiful lives, lives of never-ending fulfillment, of growth and joy, of internal peace. And isn't that what most of us are searching for?

Internal peace and, therefore, Internal Power, is an entirely personal statement of your own design. No one can provide it for you. You obtain such lasting peace only when you go within and choose it of free will. Choice is your ultimate freedom — not external choices of events outside yourself, but rather, internal choice of your thoughts and perspectives on life. It is your choice to live joyfully or sadly, happily or angrily, in love or in hate, because your perspective is always but a thought in your mind.

Choice provides us with a powerful opportunity, translating directly to an Internal Power that intensifies our strength within. Conscious thinking affords us the opportunity to recognize what kinds of thoughts we have been living by. When we begin to see how many negative thoughts we have throughout the day, we may be astonished. Many of these thoughts have controlled major aspects of our lives. To persevere to total conscious thought, we will have to do some work and recognize many things that have led us to where we are today. The journey begins with our commitment to choice.

Responsibility

Who is really responsible for our lives? Our husbands, wives, boyfriends, girlfriends, lovers, bosses, parents, society, God? Don't *we* take an active part in our daily activities, consciously or otherwise? Don't we have some kind of thought before we act, whether we are conscious of it or not? This is a crucial concept to recognize: We have the ability to control our every thought and therefore our every action. In fact, we do control every thought; however, it is often done unconsciously. Aren't we then, from a thought perspective, totally responsible for our lives?

We are the ones
responsible for our lives.

Would we rather continue through life having many random reactive thoughts? Or, would we rather have conscious control over our thoughts and our actions? There are multiple ways we can view every situation or experience. Our perspective can be changed, if we want to change it. We can view a tragedy as an opportunity, if we desire to. Instead of viewing a situation as a struggle, we can change our perspective to see it as a challenge. We can choose higher, more loving responses at every point, if we want to!

We control the feeling of victimhood within our minds. How we live and what we do with our lives are solely at our discretion. Events that have shaped us may have happened at a very early age, long before we were physically or mentally prepared to deal with them. However, we do have this moment *right now*. It is the only moment we ever have, and we are responsible for how we view it.

Choice and responsibility. What people do with their lives has an impact on themselves as well as on the people and the environment around them. This impact can have a wonderful effect, when people choose to be compassionate, caring, and loving in their every action. When people choose to be hateful, angry, wasteful, and harmful, however, this, too, has impact.

Why does one person lose a loved one in an accident and feel total forgiveness and understanding, yet another person carries hatred, anger, and an unforgiving view? Why does one person accept a diagnosis of cancer as a blessing and another as a spiteful, punishing act of God? One person takes responsibility for the thoughts and consciously chooses to take a more positive, loving approach. The other becomes mired in negativity and refuses to interrupt the stream of these thoughts long enough to acknowledge them and invoke choice.

Have you ever wanted something in life and wanted it strongly enough to receive it? Your thought process did it; you had to want it enough to do what it took to get it. You took responsibility for yourself and chose a stream of thoughts that brought you what you wanted.

Why is one person an unemployed high-school dropout while another works two jobs, starts a family, and gets a college education at night? Why do we pursue war rather than peace? Why do we argue rather than discuss and help one another? It's a matter of choice. Who is responsible for these choices? Each of us.

Because we can consciously choose our thoughts, we are responsible for our lives. If we remain unconscious of our thoughts, we are still responsible, for we made our choice to have unconscious thoughts. It is up to each of us to recognize and embrace the responsibility of our lives. No one has ever had, or ever will have, dominion over our thoughts except ourselves.

Intent

If we pause and listen to our thoughts, and if we understand we are always responsible for our thoughts, then we must also consider and comprehend our intent behind those thoughts. What is intent? Is it a moral, spiritual, or societal issue? Is it a political or business issue?

Let's look at an example of intent. If a clerk at a store gives us more money in change than is due, our intent will determine our thought processes at that moment and the subsequent choices we make. Several scenarios are possible. One, we may not check the change at all and, therefore, never detect the overage. No thoughts concerning the excess money are involved in this situation. Assuming we never catch the error, this scenario doesn't appear to involve our intent. Yet aren't we responsible for our finances?

Two, we check the change and realize, while we are still with the clerk, that the change is more than it should be. We may think, "Should I say something and give the extra money back, or keep it?" Here we enter the realm of responsibility and intent. What do we do? We may choose to justify the extra money as cash from "above" or as a discount on our purchases. We may even decide that it was supposed to happen because the store has treated us poorly.

Again, is this a moral, political, societal, or business issue? In some ways, depending on our view, it could be all of these. What do we do? What feels right? Keeping the

money may feel right at first. If we spend a lot of time justi-
fying this process, however, the guilt may catch up with us.
Would our decision be different if we found out that the
clerk would lose his or her job because the cash drawer
doesn't balance? Would it make a difference if that person
was a wealthy store owner or a struggling store owner, a sin-
gle parent with three children all dependent on that income?
Tough issues. Or are they?

In another scenario, we receive the change and don't
notice the extra amount. When we get home, however, we
find that we have an extra ten dollars. We realize we were
given the extra money at our last stop. We take a moment to
listen to our thoughts and acknowledge them consciously.
We then make a choice based on our intent as to what we
will do.

We are totally responsible for our thoughts, and we
alone govern our intent. What is your intent behind your
thoughts? What is your intent for the direction you want your
life to move in? These are important concepts to consider
and to periodically reconsider.

Intent works alongside every thought you have. You
cannot have choice without intent. You cannot have intent
without responsibility. All three occur hand-in-hand at all
times. Think of the potential ramifications when you allow
unconscious negative thoughts and emotions to run rampant
in your mind, and then consider what you could accomplish
by using conscious thought and choice. It is up to you, for it
is always a thought. Choice, responsibility, and intent —
these three very powerful concepts can propel you to vast
new heights of Internal Power.

SUMMARY

In the first doorway, Choice, we explored an exciting concept that we can incorporate into our lives. We can learn to pay attention to our positive and negative thoughts and emotions. We can take conscious control over our lives and become all that we want to be. All it requires is our desire and our willingness.

When do you begin this process? You can begin any time you want to. Because this is a lifelong process and the only "real" moment you have is right now, consider beginning right here and right now.

Stop and reflect. What do you have to do to start the thought process necessary to get you where you want to be? What kinds of thoughts have been holding you back? What kinds of limiting thoughts do you currently have?

If you have placed limits on yourself, you can remove them. You can acknowledge all your thoughts and choose to change any thoughts you wish. And as you choose the thoughts that relate to your dreams and higher desires, you will begin to experience those realities. You will experience them first in your thoughts, and then, knowing what you want in life, you can use choice of thought to get you there!

The first step in the Internal Power transformation process is choice: choose Life, a life worth living.

PLAYTIME

Project 1

For this activity use pencil and paper, a tape recorder, or even a friend. For fifteen seconds write or speak absolutely every thought that comes to mind. Do this regardless of whether your thoughts make any sense or not. Just speak or write as fast as they come up.

Listen to your thoughts on the tape recorder, read them from your paper, or discuss them with a friend. Look for themes of negative or positive statements. Are they potentially emotion-based or just statements of fact? How do you feel about these thoughts? What can you determine about your thoughts from this activity?

Try this again for a one-minute period.

Project 2

Sit in a room by yourself, where you will be uninterrupted, secure, and comfortable. For ten minutes, pay attention to your thoughts. Just let them flow in and out. Try not to focus on any thought, but allow all of them to pass through. Make a little mental note of what kinds of thoughts you are having. Positive or negative? Emotional or not? After ten minutes, decide what kinds of thoughts were represented. How are these thoughts affecting your life right now?

Project 3

Sit in a room quietly and again pay attention to your thoughts. This time, however, recognize that you can have a choice of thoughts and that you are responsible for them. Now, every time you have a negative thought you don't wish to have, let it flow through you and immediately replace it with a positive, loving thought. Do this for as long, and as often, as you like.

When you feel comfortable with this project, try it throughout a normal day. Stop your thoughts when you realize you are unaware of what you are thinking, then implement the same process. With practice you will soon find that when a troublesome situation arises, especially a traumatic one that requires solid decisions, you will be ready to tackle it through conscious choice.

Doorway Two:
Communication

A VISUALIZATION

We move across our Grand Hallway to the next door, a fine surface of painted wood. It radiates its own color, just like the walls of the hallway do. Above the door, a transom of frosted glass that dances with flashes of color catches our eye. We wonder what to expect. The Golden Key that will turn the lock and reveal the contents of this room is in our possession. We put the key in the slot. The tumbler clicks into place and we turn the knob silently. Our excitement builds as we gently push the door open to see the interior, a grand and wonderful room filled with light and sound. The many sounds immediately surround us and warmly invite us to explore further.

We briefly pause at the entrance, wondering how so many sounds can be so harmonious. With such a variety of pitches, dynamic ranges, and varying tempos, we would think it would be chaotic noise. The exquisite melody, however, is triumphant. We drift toward the center of the room, close our eyes, and feel the vibrations tingling through our bodies. A sense of peace comes over us.

Bathed in a warm light, we allow the music to flow through us. As the melodies move into our minds, we discern sounds becoming ever more distinct. The sounds emanate from everywhere in the room, and we realize they are individual messages. It is calming to hear these powerful messages.

The messages do not feel overwhelming, but instead are mesmerizing as we hear the many tones of music become distinct words. Does the communication in our lives flow this easily? Do we send harmonious tones when we communicate with others? What about the communication we receive? Is it similar? These questions quickly disappear as we continue to be entranced by the angelic sounds.

This room is the gift of communication.

COMMUNICATION

Each of us has a power that allows us to share everything we experience, know, and imagine. That power is communication — our ability to relate to everyone and everything around us. Whether we whistle tunes, speak to friends, wave our hands, or write letters, we are using our power to communicate. We also communicate to ourselves through our internal messages and inner dialogues. The source of this power comes from the energy of our thoughts. When we share our thoughts we energize our world; it is through communication that we convey our Internal Power.

Many of us are not aware of this power. We often limit our perspectives of communication merely to the verbalizing process we use in conversation. Yet, communication is so much more than that. It is our ability to express our thoughts and our opportunity to live! This impact is felt by others who experience our communication as well as by ourselves. Depending on what form — or combination of forms — we use to communicate a thought, we amplify or diminish our intended messages. These messages are colored by our self-perspectives and by the perspectives of others.

When we communicate our thoughts,
we are literally broadcasting the thoughts
and feelings we have at that moment.

Why do we communicate? It is our way of interacting with ourselves and others, and it is how we express our thoughts to the world. Communication allows us to share our experiences. Through communication we share the beauty of life, our fears and our sorrows, our wishes, desires, hopes, and dreams. When we communicate our thoughts, we are sharing our perspectives and views, literally broadcasting the thoughts and feelings we have at that moment. When we are paying conscious attention to our thoughts and are choosing the thoughts we wish to have, we are communicating with ourselves. Then we share our thoughts and feelings with others by translating them to our outer world. This is a powerful process!

Communication has often been defined as a process in which a sender gives forth a message to an intended receiver. Although we realize that many things can affect our messages, we usually tend not to accept the responsibility if they break down. When we fail to get our messages across to other people, it is easier to blame them than to acknowledge our inefficient communication process. Average adults use more than 500 common words in their daily activities — and there are thousands of dictionary definitions for those words. No wonder much of our communication is miscommunication — our education, dialects, regional definitions, institutional jargon, cultural differences, and societal standards all influence the shades of meaning in our communication. But because it is our thoughts that we attempt to share, we must be responsible for ensuring that our thoughts are received as we want them to be.

When we expand our traditional definition of communication, we become aware that communication is truly the sharing of our thoughts. Whether as inner dialogue or as conversation, we are communicating thought. Every word we speak and every physical gesture we make have thoughts that preceded them. These thoughts have energy that either empowers our lives or depletes them. The impact we have with our communication is a direct result of this energy.

Effective communication comes from recognizing that our experiences and perspectives are different from the experiences and perspectives of others. Each model of the world is completely unique. Although we may have similar views on certain issues, these views still have different experiences, feelings, and thoughts associated with them. Even identical twins cannot share every moment in the same way. This fact is both the beauty and the challenge of life. The challenge arises when we attempt to communicate our individuality to others. Therefore, understanding how we view our lives through our thoughts, and understanding other people and their ways of thinking become the keys to effective communication.

External Processing

To better understand how we communicate — how we share our thoughts — we must first understand how we obtain and process information and experiences in our daily lives. There are three primary ways to absorb and process the information we receive: auditory processing, visual processing, and kinesthetic processing. We may use all three within our daily thought activities; however, one kind of processing will usually be dominant for each of us. Let's take a brief look at each kind.

When people receive external information through the auditory process, they tend to *hear* everything around them, even the softest noise. These people hear every detail of every conversation, sometimes even conversations they are not a part of. When someone speaks, they remember what was said. They tend to go to places and do things that enhance their auditory experiences. Auditory people focus on the sounds they hear and often become irritated by disagreeable or nagging noises.

Visual people *see* everything in life, noticing the slightest visual detail. Nothing escapes their visual perspective. They may not remember conversations, but they can tell what people were wearing and on what side their hair was parted. Visual people become absorbed in experiencing life through the process of sight. They love to see many things at once, but their desire to focus on everything at the same time can sometimes overload them.

Kinesthetic people *feel* the world around them. They tend to absorb their experiences and information through a physical process — through their bodies — and are often moved by a situation's overall experience. They can feel the warmth or coldness in another person, and they like to physically handle things to experience their essence. This physical sensation brings them vital information and experience, and they tend to dislike events that don't allow them opportunities to experience things by touch and feel.

These three processors — visual, auditory, and kinesthetic — emphasize the different ways of processing external information. For example, if a group that included all three kinds of processors went into a grocery store together, their experiences would be different. After leaving the store, auditory processors would be able to describe the conversations they heard and the kind of background music that was playing. The visual processors would be able to describe what the customers and clerks were wearing, where the products were on the shelves, and what colors were on the walls. The kinesthetic people would tell their impressions of customers, whether they were friendly and inviting or unhappy and distant. They would also describe whether there was an emotional warmth or coldness to the store, depending on how they experienced the combination of people, products, colors, and layout.

Which mode seems to be most dominant for you? To know is important, because the way you process your experiences will give you a much better understanding of how you think. In addition, by understanding the other predominant modes of processing, you can become more aware of the differences in other people, which will increase your ability and effectiveness in the communication process.

Internal Processing

We also tend to use one dominant kind of internal processing — auditory, visual, or kinesthetic — to process our thoughts. It may or may not correspond to the way we process external information. Internal auditory processors *hear* their thoughts; internal visual processors tend to *see* their thoughts in a visual way; internal kinesthetic processors tend to *feel* their thoughts and emotions. How do you tend to experience your thoughts? Is it the same way as your external process? Is it different?

The way in which we communicate our model of the world — our perspectives and views — is a result of the way in which we process our lives and our thoughts both externally and internally. When we become aware of our most dominant processing types, we can begin to work with the other modes to strengthen their use in our lives, enhancing our experiences and helping us to better understand others.

FOUR METHODS OF COMMUNICATION

We communicate in four basic ways. First, we communicate our thoughts both internally and externally. Both methods take on many distinct forms. Internal communication — like dialogue, remembered phrases, songs, and emotional responses — goes on continuously in the form of thoughts. External communication includes speaking to others, writing, singing aloud, whistling, and many other ways in which we relate to the world through words and sounds.

In addition, we also communicate in a physical and nonphysical sense. We often ignore these forms of communication, even though they are both powerful communication processes. Physical forms include how we sit or stand, how we walk, where we look, our physical gestures, and even the routines we follow in our daily lives. Nonphysical means of communication, perhaps the least understood and yet frequently the most observable by others, incorporate forms of what we *don't* do: not showing up at an appointment, for example, or not picking up after ourselves at a picnic.

How we communicate internally, externally, physically, and nonphysically makes a tremendous difference in who we are and what we experience in life. And these methods often are combined to form even greater patterns of communication, becoming intense and accurate representations of our thoughts. They have great positive or negative influence, depending on the kind of thought energy we are using at the time. Our messages are powerful influences, and, just like making choices in our thinking, we can learn skills to develop and fine-tune our multiple communication processes. Let's look at all four processes in more detail.

Internal Communication

Internal communication is the process of thinking within, the thought dialogue we have within ourselves. The way we speak to our inner selves and share our thoughts within has impact and energy and affects our other forms of communication. How we choose to communicate to ourselves determines how we present our thoughts to others and the effects we will have in empowering our lives — or in not empowering them — through all forms of communication.

Internal communication is one area we can become immediately aware of, and in doing so we begin the process of developing our Internal Power. If we pause for a moment and listen to our thoughts, we start to recognize what we are saying to ourselves. For example, do you frequently say, "I never seem to do anything right," or "I can be so dumb at times," or "I never have enough time to do what I want," allowing your thoughts to unconsciously bring you down? Don't you deserve to feel better about yourself? Do you really want to label yourself so negatively? When we have such thoughts, we not only feel them internally but we communicate the same energy to our outer worlds. After all, we are what we think.

We are what we think.

For example, let's say we view ourselves as not being athletic or physically coordinated. In other words, our thoughts relating to our belief that we do not have the required physical speed, agility, balance, and grace continue to be limited. What will these thoughts do to us? How will such continuing internal communication affect us?

At first we may not even be aware of our thoughts concerning our athletic prowess, that is, we may actually communicate this attitude internally without consciously recognizing our thoughts. This internal negative thought process may go on for an extended period; eventually, we will become conscious of it. Oddly, we will probably continue these limiting dialogues with ourselves, knowingly carrying on this communication process even when we are aware of what we are saying and its potential impact upon us. In fact, we may begin to consciously use these thoughts as a way to avoid athletic-type events. This way of thinking perpetuates the cycle: We fail to gain athletic experience because we avoid athletic events.

Eventually, we find ourselves being awkward and clumsy even when we are perfectly capable of doing better, and we refuse to undertake anything that appears difficult or seems to require athletic prowess or grace. Because we believe we cannot be athletic or graceful, we begin to make statements to others about it. Others pick up on our communication and affirm it back to us in their communication, which further reinforces our limiting thought pattern. At some point, we may finally realize that these thoughts are in fact causing us to repeat the same actions over and over.

If we decide to choose a different approach, we can

begin to change our internal communication and alter our limiting beliefs. We can choose to be athletic and graceful at everything we attempt to do, first in our minds through our thoughts and ultimately in our external, physical reality. Over time the new dialogue of thought will become a part of us, and we will experience a new way of life. When we replace every negative limiting thought with a new, positive thought, we begin to see ourselves as capable and athletic. We will begin to do things that require athletic ability. We no longer will fear the outcome, but will enjoy the experience instead.

This shift occurs over time, but with conscious choice of thought we can make it stick, and we will find that we can do many athletic things with ease, grace, and ability. Just as a true athlete prepares for an event, we can begin to visualize our success and strengthen our belief in our ability through new, conscious thoughts.

What changes our physical abilities? Our bodies reflect only what we are thinking. Our bodies, like our brains, are capable of far more than we currently use. The difference between an athletic person and a nonathletic person is primarily in the thought processes. When we shift our thinking, it will reflect in our bodies. We will also begin to receive external communication from others that validates our new thinking.

Stop and listen to your internal communication. Make the changes in the perception of yourself in your thoughts, and they will be reflected in every area of your life. If you believe in your abilities and affirm that you are positive, talented, and expansive, you will begin to experience these new thoughts in your physical reality. This is Internal Power.

What other kinds of messages do we give ourselves? What do we tell ourselves when we make a mistake? What do we think about ourselves? Do we attempt to shift our focus by blaming others? What about when we look in the mirror? What kinds of thoughts do we have about our bodies? Will a diet or exercise help us, for example, if our internal thoughts continue to say that we are overweight? To experience our Internal Power, we must recognize the power of our thoughts and the constant stream of messages we have inside. As we become aware of these thoughts, we can actively change them and positively affirm better things for ourselves. We can learn how to use positive acceptance in our thoughts. After all, we learned how to use negative thoughts, didn't we? We can just as easily learn positive ones.

External Communication

When we use external communication, we express our thoughts into the world around us. Whether we are writing a letter, singing a song, discussing an issue with a friend, or even paying a bill, we are communicating our thoughts. In this wondrous process, we literally expend energy to bring our thoughts into physical reality; the words in our thoughts are translated into forms that others may experience. This is a tremendous opportunity to communicate our Internal Power.

Our external communication is a reflection to others of who and what we are at any moment. It isn't just the words we say, write, or somehow express externally, but the energy of our thinking processes that has the ultimate impact. If we feel down or depressed and our thoughts are unusually limiting, we show this energy level to others. Even if we attempt to mask our low feelings with upbeat and happy words, the low energy comes through. When our internal thoughts are positive, we clearly communicate this powerful energy externally as well.

External communication has a fascinating quality about it: we often attract similar communication back to ourselves. If we become irritated over a situation, for example, we'll often notice that others around us begin to express their irritation and unhappiness. If we become angry with someone, we will probably receive an angry reaction back from the other person. It is just the same with happy, peaceful, and joyous energy. When we whistle a happy tune, we convey our thoughts, and people that we interact with tend to reflect this happiness back. Think of the effect we have on people who are not directly involved in our communication process, yet are experiencing it because they are near us. We definitely have impact!

External communication carries with it a sense of responsibility. We can stop and reflect, even for a moment, to determine what kinds of energies we will convey in our communication with others. We must also consider our intended audience as well as those who may receive our communication indirectly. It is up to each of us to ensure that our thought energy is used in the highest and best way.

Physical Communication

We deliver a vast number of messages through our bodily postures and physical movements. Our bodies frequently reflect the true thoughts we have within, even if our verbal messages convey something different. Many of us are unaware of the physical attributes of the communication process. We often don't recognize our bodily reactions when we communicate; in fact, we may not always perceive these subtle movements in other people when they are communicating with us. The physical gestures we use express and amplify our thoughts. It is important to acknowledge and understand the physical communication we use, for it makes a difference in our ability to fully and effectively communicate our thoughts.

Why is the physical aspect of our communication so important? The way in which we carry our bodies, hold our arms and hands, use facial expressions, and so on can accentuate and illustrate our messages. At other times, our physical behavior can completely negate our intended messages. For instance, if we are engaged in a discussion with another person and move around, lose eye contact, or keep a distance, what happens to the effect of our communication? What contrary communication do we convey?

Unless we learn to become conscious of our physical actions, they may happen without our notice. When our physical presentations have contradicted our intended messages, we may experience reactions that are far different from what we had intended. If we don't usually recognize the importance of our physical communication, we often shift blame to other people for not having paid adequate attention. But the responsibility for our communication remains with us. We need to make ourselves aware of our physical communication and ensure that it is congruent with our verbal communication.

We frequently, for example, fold our arms across our chests. When we are not engaged in a communication process, this position tends to be comfortable. But when we are speaking or listening, this position is a powerful stance that wordlessly states, "I am closed off to this communication process." We are physically portraying our inner thoughts of how we feel. The way we place our bodies in relation to another, the way we make eye contact, how and where we sit — all make a great impact upon our communication.

A facial gesture can express a thousand unspoken words. The face is one of the most potent sources of physical communication and is also one of the greatest energizers of thought. We can empower any message by the expression we use, and we can also detract from our communication by exhibiting incompatible facial gestures.

How we dress, how we move, how we conduct our daily lives in a physical sense affects our communication with others as well as with ourselves. Our physical actions reflect our inner thoughts and either enhance the power of the intended communication or detract from it. If we can become more aware of our physical communication, we can bring its positive potential into the communication process.

Nonphysical Communication

Nonphysical communication, or non-action, is another way in which we communicate. We may agree to meet someone at a particular place and time, and then choose not to show up or to even call. This sends out a powerful message to others. Even though there is a lack of physical communication, there is still nonphysical communication in what we *don't* do.

Nonphysical communication is also an important element in our internal dialogue. What happens when we continuously tell ourselves about actions we will undertake and then never do them? We may tell ourselves, for instance, that we will get up early every morning as part of a new routine. We do it once, maybe twice, and then find numerous reasons to continue to sleep late. Or, we may internally commit to a diet or to an exercise program, and continue to affirm our desire and need to fulfill this obligation. We make these statements to ourselves, but then never begin the physical process. What are the ramifications of self-communication of this kind? How do we feel about ourselves when we continue to let ourselves down? How will this thought energy translate to other situations in our lives? What actions have we always wanted to do and yet never started?

Non-action is also

communication.

When we use our thoughts to invoke change in our lives — when we affirm a new attitude — and then begin to excuse our nonperformance and lack of physical manifestation, we literally snuff the energy from our thoughts. This communication of non-action limits our belief in our Internal Power. We curb our unlimited abilities through our limiting thoughts.

Whether we are using internal or external nonphysical communication, we are broadcasting our inner thoughts. An important element in our transformation includes understanding when we use nonphysical communication and how it affects us and others. Learning to bring our thoughts into alignment with our actions brings us closer to being our true unlimited selves.

SUMMARY

The power of our communication is vast — limitless. Whether we communicate with ourselves, other people, or the world around us, we tap our Internal Power, which derives its energy from our thoughts. Communication is a wondrous and multifaceted process that allows us to experience life in many ways. We assimilate and integrate information through an innately predominant auditory, visual, or kines thetic process. We may process our external and our internal communication using the same mode — being both an external and internal visual type, for example — or we may use different modes. We can learn to expand our ability to function with these modes and also increase our use of the other modes. More important, we can understand that each person has his or her combination of internal and external processing. This helps us understand how other people derive their models of the world and gives us the opportunity to improve our communication process with them. Recognizing other people's perspectives and acknowledging their processing modes enhance our communication with them immeasurably.

The dynamic process of communication is illustrated in the four major ways we communicate. Whether we use internal or external, physical or nonphysical communication, or any combination of these methods, we energize our lives and the lives of others. The power of our thought is felt by everyone who experiences our communication style. How we stand, what we say, the tones we use, the pauses in our messages — all will either enhance or diminish the messages we wish to relate to others. Any missing behavior, inner conflicting dialogue, and limiting beliefs will also be reflected in our communication. We must fully embrace each method, understand its use, and recognize the potency in combining several ways of communicating.

Our personal transformation and self-discovery process takes on remarkable power and growth when we fully accept our ability to communicate. As in our Choice doorway, with this ability comes responsibility. We are responsible for our thoughts and our communication, and we are also responsible for the intent behind our thoughts. We can learn to choose both appropriate thoughts and effective methods to broadcast these thoughts, and we can learn to understand other people's perspectives and modes of processing.

Stop and reflect. The power to communicate and share your thoughts gives you a beautiful opportunity to experience the richness of living. You have the unique ability to interact with all forms of life through your communication. When you choose the highest and best ways to share the thoughts and feelings you have with your outer world, you share your unlimited potential. You have the ability to share every thought, experience, dream, and desire with those around you. When you are aware of your extraordinary power to communicate effectively, you also open yourself to the power of exceptional communication from others. This is the Internal Power process. This is sharing life. This is communication.

PLAYTIME

Project 1

The next time you are in a conversation, pay special attention to your external dialogue and your physical communication. Do all the forms of your physical communication support your dialogue? Do some of your habitual physical gestures weaken your words? Do any other forms of your physical communication contradict your words?

Try to become as aware as possible of the many ways you communicate to others, nonverbally as well as verbally.

Project 2

When you are with friends or co-workers, pay attention to how they describe events and situations. Do they use visual descriptions of what they see? Do their statements reflect what they hear? Do certain people speak mainly about emotion or feelings? The things they emphasize in their conversations all relate to how they process their worlds. How do these descriptions compare with your personal processing style? Are you predominantly auditory, visual, or kinesthetic? Internally? Externally?

Project 3

Imagine what life would be like if you couldn't hear. Suppose you couldn't see? What if your ability to touch was gone? Put yourself in these situations and visualize how your model of the world would change. Do you realize any new perspectives? How does this new awareness help you to relate to other people's perspectives?

Doorway Three:
Positive Thinking

A VISUALIZATION

As we travel up our hallway, we come to the next doorway, with a door of elaborate leaded stained glass. This remarkable glasswork is in striking contrast to the other doors we have opened. The shapes and curves of the sections add to the splendor of the entry, radiating a glow like a rainbow. The delightful colors have a power and delicacy that somehow seem to smile at us. We quickly retrieve our Golden Key so we can enter through this fascinating door.

As we unlock the door and begin to push it open, beams of light shoot out through the crack. As we step gently into the room, the light bathes us in its splendor. We are drawn deeper into the room by a soft, heartwarming voice — our voice! At first we are a bit startled to hear our voice in this room, but we quickly become mesmerized by the soothing, gentle tones, and we quietly stand and listen to the sweet words. We feel positive, affirming, and accepting words penetrating and relaxing every cell of our bodies.

The experience is wonderful. We now know what it is like to feel peaceful within. We have entered the realm of Positive Thinking — our Positive Thinking — and we begin to understand what it sounds like and feels like to believe in ourselves and in our lives. We absorb the vibrations of our voices through every pore, wishing that the voice would never cease. It is as if we can become these positive thoughts, these powerful words of affirmation. We can do it right here and right now. We have the Internal Power to be loving and positive through our thoughts.

POSITIVE THINKING

Just imagine what life would be like if every thought we had, every belief we held, and every experience we encountered was positive, loving, and full of joy. We would respect and honor ourselves and would believe in our unlimited abilities. Is such a life possible? Can we ever experience such inner happiness and knowing? We can if we choose to do so. The opportunity lies in the choices of our inner thoughts. To think positively means to believe in ourselves, to accept ourselves, and to affirm the greatest good for ourselves every moment of every day. The self-discovery process is a truly beautiful internal unfolding. Like a bud coming into full bloom, each of us can unfold our inner petals of potential. This is the power of Positive Thinking, our next doorway to Internal Power.

What exactly is positive thinking? To begin with, positive thinking is a means to freedom. It is the way to free ourselves from our self-imposed bondage of limiting beliefs. To think positively is to accept ourselves at every moment just for who we are, recognizing that we are unique and that we possess unlimited abilities. We can cultivate our unlimited potential by choosing the highest and best thoughts at every moment and in every situation. We become our own best friends through the positive thinking process, and when it occurs, we become best friends to everyone and everything around us.

Positive thinking
is a means to freedom.

Positive thinking also helps us to live in the moment. When we allow the positive thinking process to energize our lives, we release our past, allow the future to unfold naturally, and reside in the only moment we have: *the now moment*. It is in the now moment that positive thoughts have their greatest energy. Positive thoughts energize us to take positive action and give us the desire to make a difference in our lives at this moment — and then we make a difference in other people's lives as well. By choosing positive thoughts we engage our respect for ourselves, our self-esteem and value, and our unlimited abilities.

Positive thinking is ultimately more than our thoughts — it is a way of life. We see the world with fresh new eyes and recognize the unlimited potential and opportunity that exist everywhere. When we see the world in this way, we allow our thoughts to expand to the reality that each of us truly has an impact in the world. We are a part of the whole process and each of us does make a difference.

Thought Perspectives

If positive thinking is so powerful, why have so many of us not embraced it as a way of life? Why do we often seem to be anxious, scared, angry, frustrated, depressed, or confused in our thoughts? Why do experiences become so overwhelming at times?

To answer these questions, we can start by understanding how our thought perspectives influence our lives. Everything we experience is based on our perceptions and evaluations. These perspectives come from our beliefs, experiences, awareness, memories, teachings, and understanding. We also hold visions, dreams, desires, and hopes for the future. These various perspectives are all thoughts. Because we can choose the thoughts we wish to have, we can also transform our perspectives, if we so desire. This shifting of our thoughts will change our experience of life. We can move from lower thoughts — which drain us and stifle our growth and potential — to higher and more uplifting and energizing thoughts. This is our opportunity to become the unlimited beings we truly are and to create inner peace and happiness.

Shifting our thoughts
changes our experience of life.

We can take any aspect of our lives that doesn't seem to be flowing or working and turn it into a loving, peaceful, and positive experience. We can choose to see any event or situation with a positive and accepting view, or we can continue to remain helpless and unhappy with the situation we are in. Change, if it is to happen, occurs first within our thought processes.

We have all encountered consistently happy and confident people, who believe in themselves and the world around them and see the good in their lives and in the lives of others. We enjoy being around them — they help us feel good. They consciously choose to find the very best in everything. To them joyful living is a way of life.

We have also all been around unhappy, gloomy people. We quickly recognize these kinds of people because they are so wrapped up in their cynicism and negative, unhappy thinking that they do not radiate any positive energy or uplift us in any way when we are in their presence. They often choose to find the absolute worst in everyone and everything. They like to blame their bad fortune on others and on society in general, and they tend to have an excuse for everything. They project their internal negative thoughts toward everyone they come in contact with, and then those emotions are magnetized right back to them through their physical reality. Bad things seem to find them.

What is the biggest difference between these two kinds of people? It is in their way of thinking and relating to life. Happy people have a constant stream of positive thoughts; gloomy people allow their emotional baggage, limiting beliefs, and unhappy thoughts to control them.

At times throughout our lives, we experience both thought perspectives. We can move along a continuum from unhappy and gloomy to happy and confident, depending on where we are and what we perceive is happening to us in our daily experiences. What causes these mood shifts? Is it our daily reality and external events that cause the swings in our attitudes toward life, or is it the way we perceive events and people? What brings these differences in thought and how do we change our perspectives to get the most out of our lives? The difference comes from the way we think.

Limited and Unlimited Thinking

When we think positively, what tends to happen? What do we usually experience when we are feeling good and everything seems to be going smoothly? When our lives are flowing, we feel wonderful mentally and physically. We recognize our abilities. We can conquer everything life has to offer. We are unlimited. Nothing seems to get in our way, or if something does, we attend to it and keep going. However, what happens to us the rest of the time? Things begin to fall apart. Everything seems to become an enormous hurdle. Life becomes a struggle. We are blocked. Our bodies and our minds seem to freeze up at the same time. We become tired, unhappy, and depressed and begin to blame the world for our misfortune. What has happened to us? Why can we feel so great at one point and so down the next?

What we focus our thoughts on will determine the reality we experience. When we focus our thoughts on past experiences and memories that are emotionally charged with the negative energies of fear, hurt, anger, sadness, anxiety, judgment, or guilt, we are literally re-living our past negative experiences and are bringing negative emotional energy into our current reality. Regardless of whether we are focusing on past fears and adverse thoughts or are projecting these fears into our future, the results will be the same. We are limiting ourselves. Negative thought is limiting thought. Limiting thoughts consume our energy rather than provide us with energy.

On the other hand, if we focus on satisfying and happy past experiences and memories — on positive thoughts — we allow our current perspectives to be charged with energies of satisfaction, happiness, love, beauty, harmony, and kindness. Focusing these thought energies into our perceived future can project the necessary uplifting energy to create the reality we imagine and desire.

Through positive thinking we choose thoughts that express our beliefs in our abilities and self-worth. We engage the energy of these thoughts to create the reality we want right now. This is unlimited thinking. Positive thought is unlimited thought. When we use positive thinking, when we choose to affirm the best for ourselves, we find we have an unlimited supply of energy.

Positive thought
is unlimited thought.

If negative thoughts are limited and positive thoughts are unlimited, does this mean that one is bad and the other good? Is one kind wrong and the other right? No, for each kind of thought provides us with an opportunity to grow. If we are thinking positively, we are already pursuing life in an unlimited and abundant fashion. We can continue to add to this perspective by challenging ourselves to newer and higher unlimited awareness and thought. If, however, we recognize a negative thinking process occurring, we have a wonderful opportunity to acknowledge the limiting perspectives of our past and release them. When we do, we can replace the negative, limiting thoughts with unlimited positive thoughts. Without negative thoughts, we would not have a basis for comparison. Without positive thoughts, we would not have energizing thoughts to uplift us. Both kinds of thoughts, negative and positive, provide us with choices.

The key to choosing our thoughts is to learn how to recognize the different kinds of thoughts. To do this, we need to know how both unlimiting positive and limiting negative thoughts feel to us.

How do unlimiting positive thoughts energize us? When we are excited and happy about life, what kinds of thoughts do we tend to have? Do our positive thoughts give us the desire to do things? Do these thoughts give us the energy necessary to act on them?

Our negative thoughts also have their own energy. How do we feel, both physically and mentally, when we are engaged in limiting thought? What fears do we begin to perpetuate and project elsewhere? How have negative thoughts controlled us in the past? When negative thoughts begin to direct our lives, do we affirm and believe in our abilities? Negative thoughts are limiting and cannot provide the energy to lift us back up. Instead, negative thoughts continue to spiral like a whirlpool, pulling us in deeper and deeper, until we break the cycle with positive and unlimited thought. Then through our conscious choice of thought, we can reverse the cycle and bring our thoughts back up to an unlimited awareness. This is the Internal Power of positive thinking.

The Sources of Our Perspectives

Why do we sometimes turn to lower, more limiting negative thoughts even when we are trying to focus on positive thoughts? Perhaps something within our experience triggers a negative memory or we tap into a perspective that has negative thought energy associated with it. These thoughts may surface from some past emotion that we perceived as real or even just imagined. Or, we may have accepted as our view a belief or teaching from another person. We may never have even experienced the emotion firsthand. Instead, someone else may have experienced it and we accepted that version as our own.

We may feel limiting emotions of anger, fear, guilt, anxiety, frustration, or sadness. If we never released those emotional thoughts when we encountered them, they will remain within our memories, charged and ready to go, waiting for their chance to come back and "help" us in similar circumstances by energizing comparable situations we are facing. But do negative thoughts really help? When we focus on past negative perspectives, we bring their limiting energies into our current situations.

We can draw upon past positive, unlimited perspectives the same way and tap into past experiences that are charged with satisfaction and unlimited positive emotions. We can also use affirmations as a way to trigger our positive awareness in our current perspectives. When we have and use thoughts that are positive, we empower ourselves with their innate energy, and flow easily and effortlessly through life.

Often the most prevalent source of past thought perspectives is from our childhoods. When we are young we seek approval from others, and we look to our families, teachers, and friends to show us right from wrong, good from bad. We look at other people's models of the world to use as frameworks to create our own. We look for love. Our curiosity and thirst for knowledge brings us to numerous experiences that challenge us to understand life.

When we are faced with significant situations that we are unprepared for, we often run to the comfort of other people and look for their guidance. We experience situations from standpoints of limited wisdom and experience, and we rely heavily on other people to be our role models. Depending on our thoughts and feelings at the time, we frequently accept the views of others, and we allow another's perspective to become our reality. This occurs especially in our childhood, because we tend to mirror other behaviors in an attempt to learn what is appropriate for us. How different life would be if we thoroughly understood our unlimited abilities and were constantly encouraged to use them.

The views and beliefs we accept take on powerful energies, both positive and negative. As we create our standards, beliefs, understanding, and experiences, we build foundations for our adult perspectives. The perspectives we create in our childhoods can become either stumbling blocks or power boosters later in life. If we perceive that we stumbled over an event in our youth, we may continue to stumble over it throughout our lives. If we felt we succeeded, this thought perspective will energize us in our adult lives. In either case, because the events are from our past, the only connection we have to them now is through our thoughts. The energies that we associate with past negative perspectives are what we seek to understand and release.

Let's suppose, for example, that as children we made mistakes that adults punished us for, either physically or verbally. At such an early age, we may believe that adults have the highest understanding and that punishment is necessary. If we are confident and recognize our inner abilities, we release the situation and move on. However, if we continue to associate mistakes with punishment, we imagine and embrace this hurt perspective and retain its thought energy. We may spend the rest of our lives assuming that all mistakes are bad and that we will be punished in some way for them. We begin to fear the punishment that may happen from making a mistake.

We may not be aware of these thoughts or of their connections to the past; we simply feel that mistakes are wrong and are to be avoided completely. As adults, we stop taking risks. When we do make mistakes, we look to our past and bring negative thought energy into our current moment. When we do, we limit ourselves by not allowing positive and higher awareness into the moment.

What we needed to know about mistakes in childhood is what we still need to understand now: that *mistakes are okay*. We learn and grow from mistakes we make; that is their usefulness and power. We can choose our thoughts so that we view mistakes positively, and we can affirm our ability to take risks and succeed. This process is completely up to us. We cannot blame the people in our past for their negative influence — they did the best they could given what they knew at the time. We also cannot feel guilty or judge ourselves for our perceived inabilities or wrongdoings in our childhoods. We can, however, change our current thought perspectives in this moment.

> *We learn and grow from*
> *the mistakes we make, and that*
> *is their usefulness and power.*

How many of our childhood experiences are we still engaging in as adults? How many beliefs have we accepted from other people that truly do not reflect our own, yet we continue to accept them? When we are faced with events in life that seem overwhelming and we feel powerless to overcome them, we often become frustrated, confused, hurt, and angry. Whether we are children or adults, when we feel powerless we frequently become reactive rather than proactive. This comes from our limiting beliefs. When we feel we don't have the wisdom or knowledge to overcome the hurdles we face, we allow negative thoughts to control our thought processes. But we can take responsibility for our lives and choose to think in unlimited and positive ways, turning around any situation and seeing it in a positive light. We have everything we need right now to handle anything we face in life. We have our unlimited selves.

AFFIRMATIONS

Most of our thought perspectives come from our external search for love, understanding, wisdom, and peace. This process starts in our youth when we seek external positive affirmation and acceptance from other people. What we are really looking for, however, is for our inner thoughts to be acknowledged and accepted by ourselves. Yet, how many of us as adults still seek external approval and affirmation? We create unbalanced relationships in an attempt to provide this external illusion of acceptance. We fill up our lives with material objects as a way to fill the void we feel within our own thoughts.

Ironically, we cannot truly receive affirmation and approval externally until we embrace ourselves internally. We can experience a positive and peaceful life only when we bring these positive perspectives into our thoughts. By focusing our thoughts on our inner unlimited abilities, we engage the positive thinking process in our lives and thereby release the need for external affirmation.

You create the opportunities for satisfaction and joy in your life. If you think positive thoughts and have an upbeat perspective, you will experience this reality both internally and externally. For instance, if you begin a conversation by saying you are delighted or satisfied with something, the discussion magically starts on a cheerful note. When others around you are gloomy or negative, you can maintain your positive momentum. Even the most negative people will become more upbeat, or they will quickly move on.

Each of us deserves to feel happy, content, peaceful,

and positive. When we have a positive perspective inside, we create the external mirror in our physical reality. We cannot look to other people and things to provide this perspective for us, for the external never will provide it until we feel it within. We may, at times, feel a momentary happiness that we associate with another person or object, yet, in reality, our inner thoughts give us that joy.

Many of us have been given tremendous affirmation and acceptance by others; we may even have the physical proof of our abilities through numerous possessions, degrees, and awards. However, if we don't feel affirmed, accepted, and positive in our thoughts, these external messages may go completely unnoticed. When we don't believe it within our thoughts, we can't see it or hear it from the outside — a great loss of our Internal Power.

How do we gain back our Internal Power? If we don't currently have the highest and best thoughts within, or don't think positively at the moment, what can we do to tap the energy of positive thinking? We tap this powerful energy by affirming ourselves. We become aware, through conscious choice of thought, that we are unique, special, and unlimited. We focus our thoughts on the positive statements we can make about ourselves. We make the internal commitment to get the most out of every moment through positive thinking, and we remove our self-imposed limiting beliefs by replacing those thoughts with unlimited perspectives.

Ways to Affirm

The power of positive thinking can be easily engaged by using positive affirmations. These affirmations are the highest and most unlimited statements we can make about ourselves. They are expressions of our unlimited abilities. We charge our lives with the energy these affirmations provide, and actually change our lives.

How do we create and use affirmations? Affirmations can be done in many ways. We can verbalize these positive statements, write them down, visualize them, or just take time out to think about them. Regardless of the form they take, we must make them as unlimiting and energizing as we can. These statements are meant to engage and remind us of our unlimited abilities and potential -- our Internal Power.

Affirmations have a unique and powerful quality: They are able to cancel the effects of negative thoughts or perspectives. Every time we recognize negative thoughts or situations occurring, we can choose positive affirmations to immediately put alongside them. These positive thoughts effectively cancel out the negative energy and provide us with unlimited opportunity. Every positive thought we have releases negativity. When we choose to become conscious of our thoughts, this process begins to work. In a short time the positive thinking process becomes a way of life.

What can we positively affirm? To begin with, we can affirm the miracle of our existence. We deserve to have everything we want in life, and affirmations help us to acknowledge this fact. Each of us is a very special person, and our lives have impact in this world. We need to affirm our unlimited abilities, affirm that we can create any reality we desire.

Let's look at a few examples of affirmations.

I believe in myself and my unlimited capabilities.

I think in positive and unlimited ways.
I deserve to follow my dreams and enjoy life to the fullest.
I love myself unconditionally.
I can overcome anything that life brings me.
I have everything I need right at this moment.
I respect all my abilities.
I acknowledge and release my past with dignity and gratitude.

What if we don't believe these positive statements? How can we honestly think or write an affirmation that we feel is not true? Won't this send out mixed messages in our thoughts? On the contrary, if we currently feel down and limited, this is the ideal time to uplift and validate ourselves with positive affirmations. These unlimited thoughts provide the energy to break the negative cycle and turn our thoughts around. Because we have only the *now moment* to physically do things, the only way we can create a positive moment and a future positive perspective is by affirming ourselves now. Our future is created by the choices of thoughts we make right now.

There are several ways we can help ourselves trigger these unlimited thoughts. These few tools can go a long way to assist us in our personal transformation:

(1) *Affirmation statements.* Write affirmation statements on little pieces of paper, and place them around your home and office. Any space you regularly use becomes a good spot to remind you of your unlimited abilities. To maintain this dynamic positive energy, change the thoughts frequently and

write out new affirmations to replace the current ones. These constant reminders provide you with numerous opportunities to affirm yourself in your thoughts.

(2) *Affirmation sheets.* Take a few minutes out of your busy schedule to affirm in writing all your unlimited thoughts. Writing out affirmations in a continuous process enables your unlimited thoughts to unfold as you go. Each thought builds to newer and higher awareness. If a negative or limiting thought surfaces, write that down and then immediately release it by affirming yourself with the next positive statement. Write for as long as you wish. The statements do not need to be long, just positive and uplifting.

(3) *A journal.* A powerful way to grow is to keep a journal or diary. It can include your affirmations, along with creative ideas, personal dialogue, chronological events, and numerous other thoughts. Many people already keep journals; you can make them far more, however, than just daily recitals of events. You can often break up negative thinking by writing all the thoughts you have; as you write and affirm, you begin to shift your focus from a negative to a positive perspective, energizing yourself. If you feel that a journal takes too much time and energy, remember that you are in total control of your life, and can create as much time and energy as you need for anything you want. You can also remove any personal expectations of how often to write and how much to cover in your journal.

(4) *Verbalize affirmations.* Verbalizing positive affirmations is a powerful way to experience new perspectives, and it often assists others in their positive growth as well. You

can affirm yourself and others at the same time, and no longer need to be stifled by becoming involved in negative conversations. When you affirm your beliefs verbally, you quickly learn to distinguish your thoughts from the influences of others.

(5) *Affirmations on tape.* When you verbalize your affirmations on tape, you hear your own voice and can doubly feel these affirmations. This is especially helpful for times when you are down and limited in your thoughts. A tape of positive affirmations can help shift your focus more easily. After listening to your voice reminding you of your unlimited potential, you can follow with new affirmations that you write or verbalize. Numerous professional cassette tapes are also available with affirmations and thoughts on positive thinking.

(6) *"Time out."* Another enjoyable and fascinating way to do affirmations is by visualizing and focusing your thoughts during a brief meditation or "time out." Take a few minutes to find a comfortable spot where you will not be interrupted. Play some soft music if you wish; relax your body and then your mind, and let yourself begin to visualize your true unlimited potential. If negative thoughts bubble up, let them quickly flow through. Continue your positive focus. Daydream about all the things you want to experience in life. Focus your thoughts on the positive things you have created in the past, see your current life as being wonderful, and project those positive thoughts into your future. When you are finished, you will find a renewed positive outlook that gives you new energy and perspective.

SUMMARY

Life can be a struggle or a challenge, painful or pleasurable, difficult or effortless. It is our perspective that makes the difference, and it is the thoughts we have that give us our perspective. We are the only ones who can change these thoughts, and we have the power and opportunity to invoke conscious choice of thought at any moment we desire. We are responsible for our thoughts and, therefore, for our reality. If our current reality is less than we would like, we must focus our attention on new thoughts that are unlimited and positive, thereby engaging our Internal Power.

We are the only source of limitation in our lives, and we limit ourselves through our thoughts. When we continue to believe and act upon past negative messages, teachings, beliefs, and perspectives, we limit our potential. Negative thoughts consume our energy and keep us mired in an unhappy and unproductive moment. We have the opportunity to change this in an instant. *Stop and reflect.* We can affirm ourselves positively and call upon memories of past successes to immediately reverse our limiting thoughts. In positive thinking, there is no failure, only learning experiences.

We are the only source
of limitation in our lives.

One of the most harmful negative thoughts is fear. When we invoke fearful thoughts, we choose the limiting perspective of our inability and lack of sufficient knowledge to handle a situation. If we stop long enough to focus on the possibilities before us, we recognize that every problem has a solution, but we have to be open to ideas in order for them to surface. When we concentrate on fearful thoughts, there is no room for new and greater thoughts to come through, and so we limit our possibilities. It is often useful to bring negative thoughts to the surface in order to release them. We control our thoughts and the opportunity to change them. When our focus shifts, we shift.

The power of positive thinking is more than thought — it is a way of life. When we hold the perspective of our unlimited ability and potential, we engage the energy of these positive thoughts, which is transmitted in everything we do and to everyone we come in contact with. Our impact is felt by the world around us. When we realize and engage our Internal Power of positive thinking, we become open to all that life has to offer. We can then give out what we have within — our own Positive Thinking.

PLAYTIME

Project 1

Take ten minutes to write affirmations out on a piece of paper. Try to become aware of all your thoughts as you write, including your negative thoughts. Affirm yourself using the highest and best thoughts you can. Keep building on these affirmations until all the negative thoughts cease.

Project 2

Walk through a mall, your office, your school, or other busy area. Greet those you meet with a smile and a cheerful hello. What reactions do you receive? How does it make you feel? What impact do you have on other people's lives? On your life?

Project 3

Pay close attention to your conversations with other people. Watch for your negative statements. When you use a negative statement, release it and immediately affirm yourself positively within. Verbalize this positive thought perspective. How does it make you feel? How do other people reflect this back to you?

Doorway Four:
Creativity

A VISUALIZATION

As we move back into the hallway, Golden Key in hand, we reflect for a moment on just how powerful our minds really are. We are beginning to understand how we can tap into our source of Internal Power just by acknowledging that it exists, and that we can control our thoughts.

We walk toward the next door. Our thoughts seem to flow more easily now, as we better understand the Internal Power within. The hallway appears alive, vibrating to our enthusiastic feeling about our new lives. As we approach the next room, we notice a completely different entry than we previously experienced.

This door is wrapped with elaborate paper and ribbons — it looks just like a large present. We stand back and examine the entrance with delight. Everyone loves a present, especially a big one like this is. We use our Golden Key and enter, and we see a room filled with a multitude of objects, all wrapped like presents. We scan the room in a circular fashion; as we come back to the point where we entered, we realize that the objects we saw before have all changed. As we focus on a group of objects, they change right before our eyes!

We close our eyes, rub them for a moment, and open them. Alas, all the objects are gone and the room is completely empty, except for one wrapped box in the center of the brightly lit room. The box is wrapped exactly like the door is. What does this mean?

Somehow, the realization quietly comes to us that all the objects we saw are available to us inside the box in the center of the room. Because we have been given the gift of imagination, the only requirement to open the box and let the objects out is our creativity. We stand quietly, astonished at the power emanating from the box; it is the power of our own creative essence.

CREATIVITY

The gift of imagination is one of the most magical and exciting aspects of life. We have the power and ability to imagine anything we want. We can take a simple thought and weave an entire story from it. Our very lives are such stories — we use our imaginative thought to embark upon the journey of life, creating every step and experience as we go along. The wonder of life is in our creative ability, and we hold the key to creativity in our Internal Power.

Are all of us really creative beings? How do we define such a term as creativity? What does it mean to be creative? How can creativity lead to our Internal Power? For many of us, our creativity has been diminished, because we do not accept the fact that we are creative. In fact, most of us do not know how to describe creativity other than in artistic terms. We view artists, painters, sculptors, dancers, musicians, and the like as creative beings. However, to say that we are creative is another thing. The road to Internal Power is to understand that this creative thought energy resides within each of us *without exception*. The creative process is an enormously powerful thought energy in our lives, and we can use it every moment.

To expand our definition of creativity, let's first take a look at Webster's dictionary definition: *"the ability to produce or bring about by a course of action or behavior."* According to this definition, creativity is the *ability* to produce something. This ability is in each of us, and it lies in our imagination. Everyone has the gift of imagination. Our ability to imaginatively create comes from our ability to think.

Through our desire and willingness to hold our imaginative thought long enough, physical results are produced in our lives. If we can hold this inner vision, this imaginative thought, we can create anything we want in life. Creativity is in no way limited to the artistic arena. Creativity is the ability to imagine and hold our thoughts long enough to take physical action. Because we all have imagination, aren't we all creative? Haven't we always created what we wanted when we put our minds to it and focused our thoughts on it?

Each of us exhibits the same creative energy as do artists, sculptors, or musicians. Our thoughts lead us to create our lives just as artists' thoughts lead them to create paintings or films. To truly believe in our creativity, we must fully embrace our unlimited imagination. We must allow ourselves to recognize our endless ability to create anything we want through our imagination; then we can fully incorporate our imaginative thoughts into our lives.

Why have so many of us not seen ourselves as creative beings? Because we have been holding a definition of creativity that is far too narrow. We have viewed our daily lives as routines that are something other than creative and imaginative. Many of us have been giving away our Internal Power by accepting other people's views, labels, and definitions of our creativity. Yet, this creative thought energy is truly the driving mechanism of our lives. Preparing a meal, for example, is creative. Unless we have been trained as chefs, however, we probably don't see it that way. Even in its simplest form, the meal was first a thought in our imagination. As we imagine every detail, the meal becomes a desire we wish to fulfill. As we choose to put together the ingredients and cook them, the meal becomes a material reality.

Artists do the same thing. First they envision the subject in their imagination, then set about creating the piece of art. They make their drafts, collect their paints, decide on the proper brushes and canvas, and bring their imaginative thought into physical reality. The process is the same for a composer, a dancer, a musician, and other more commonly defined "creative" people. So is there any difference between our creativity and theirs? Not with our expanded definition. We human beings bring about things and produce things throughout our daily lives, and we constantly use our imaginative thoughts to begin the process. This is the creative process. We are all creative individuals. In fact, our creativity is quite elaborate if we consider the variety of activities we conduct in our daily lives, each requiring first a thought from our imagination.

We are all

creative individuals.

Everything that we do is first a thought in our imagination and is then carried out in its physical form if we so desire. The key to our Internal Power is to learn to stimulate our imagination and expand our lives to incorporate our unlimited creative abilities. Just think what our lives can become if we view every aspect of life from the awareness that we can create anything we want! Even acts of destruction — such as letting go of old patterns and manifestations — can be creative, for they pave the way for new imaginative thought to come through.

Creativity is the essence of our lives. We *all* have the gift of imaginative thought and are, therefore, creative beings. If we can dream it we can create it — be it a dinner, a job, a space shuttle, or a *Mona Lisa*. We can use our thoughts to create the lives we desire and the material things we want. We can become anything we put our thoughts to. After all, we have created our lives to this moment, even though we may not have been fully conscious of the creative process.

Forgotten Creativity

Why have we not understood or embraced this creative process of our imaginative thoughts if it is really so powerful? For many of us, our early attempts at using our imaginative thought may have been stifled, suppressed, or stopped altogether. We may have lost sight of our creativity at an early age when we presented mud pies and crayon wall drawings to our parents in the living room and failed to receive the positive acknowledgments we expected. This lack of affirmation does not mean that we must continue to see ourselves as noncreative or unimaginative, nor do we need to blame anyone for our lost perspective.

As children, we are totally consumed with our imagination, curiosity, and exploration of life along with our creative abilities. In addition, we look to others for affirmation and understanding, to learn right from wrong and what is acceptable and unacceptable behavior. Our guides or teachers in life, be they parents, other relatives, school teachers, friends, or peers, deal with life from their perspectives. As children, we use these people and their models of the world to learn what to do and how to act. Yet, how is a two-year-old child to know that his drawing on the wall was a great piece of art, when the parent is punishing him for his choice of location? Or, how does a student feel when the teacher gives her a low grade because textbook examples were not followed in the exact format? The child and student were looking for acceptance and approval of their creative talents, but the parent wanted to teach the child not to damage the wall, and the teacher wanted the student to follow prescribed directions.

The child may link the punishment to his creativity, not to the wall location. The student may equate the low mark to her creative abilities. In either case, the creative act is lost. It takes only a few such encounters for the child or student to forget about trying *anything* creative. No party is to blame for this situation. The key is to embrace our creativity *now*, and to encourage everyone of every age to express their creativity as well.

A different scenario may have occurred in our childhood and youth. Our parents — or teachers, peers, friends — may have positively acknowledged and affirmed our creativity from an artistic perspective. They may have assisted us in cultivating our artistic talents and supported the pursuit of painting, music, writing, and so on. We may have adopted the belief, therefore, that painting or playing an instrument was creative. We may have accepted the limited view of creativity as being solely an artistic endeavor. Perhaps no one ever pointed out that all life endeavors use creative thought as well. Balancing our checkbook or cooking a meal may not be within our adult definition of creativity, yet each of these physical acts requires our imagination and our creative process.

In each case, whether our creative efforts were stifled or whether we were encouraged to cultivate our artistic talent in a narrow range of creativity, there is no reason to blame our parents or anyone else for our feeling of lost creativity. We are responsible for our lives right here and now — past experiences are to learn from, not to hold on to. The important thing to remember is that we are *all* creative through our thoughts. Regardless of how we may have felt in an earlier time, we possess the ability to embrace and express our unlimited creativity. Creativity is part of the human experience.

Imagination

What is imagination? Where does it come from? How can we expand it in our lives? The answers to these questions will help us understand and use this powerful thought energy. As we have discussed, the creative process starts with an imaginative thought. We "image" something in our minds, forming mental pictures. The more we focus on these thoughts, the more real they become in our minds. As we continue to focus on these images, more thoughts emerge and the pictures become clearer and more defined. When we desire these images to become physical reality, we take physical action — and soon the total creative process is complete. In this way, we produce and bring about the physical things in our lives.

Our imagination is far more than just a passing fantasy: Our imagination is a wonderful potent thought energy that allows us the opportunity to visualize anything. We can experience any reality in our minds through our imagination first, and we can change our mental pictures as we go along. By focusing our imaginative thoughts on a particular person, place, thing, or event, we can run through many possibilities and scenarios. We can add to our mental images, change them, or dissolve them, which allows us to create the ideal vision of something and then begin the process to bring this mental image into physical reality. Even as we take the appropriate steps to create this reality, our imaginative thoughts allow us to continue to modify the image so that we can choose, if we wish, to create that image in the form of its highest potential.

Our imagination is a wonderful
potent thought energy that allows
us to visualize anything.

How do you expand your imagination into every part of your life? If you can accept your unlimited potential to imagine, you will begin to generate new ideas through your imagination and focus on your mental images long enough to allow these thoughts to expand. Take these inspiring ideas and images that seem to momentarily pass through your thoughts and capture them. When you hold these imaginative possibilities longer than an instant, you can seize their unlimited potential and begin to work with the thoughts. How many thoughts race through your mind now, only to disappear as fast as they came?

Our physical reality comes from our ability to capture our imaginative thoughts, play with them and expand them, and then use our desire and willpower to manifest them in the best and most useful ways possible. So how do we expand our imagination? We learn how to embrace and use our imagination through our daily conscious use and acknowledgment of it.

Creativity in Our Daily Lives

Let's look at areas of our lives in which we use imagination and the creative process. One immediate question is, "How are we creative in the things we do each day if our daily lives are just routine?" Consider this: The very nature of a routine is a creative experience. Although we are choosing a structured, repetitive thought process, it does not lessen the fact that it is creative. Besides, how did these routines start? Have we swayed even slightly from them? Are the events in our daily routines ever exact carbon copies of the day before? Doesn't it require a fair amount of thought to stay within a structured routine? We are constantly using our imagination and the creative process in all facets of our lives.

(1) *Home life.* Where is our creativity hiding at home? Every completed chore or household responsibility is really an imaginative thought carried out. What would happen if we changed our perspectives on our thoughts? What if we viewed housework, household responsibilities, and even our homes as creative expressions? The lawn is a vehicle to create a natural lush carpet around our homes. We use our imagination to create mental visions of large, perfectly shaved green grass rugs surrounding our homes. Garden plots become our exquisite canvases to paint dazzling flower arrangements or an exotic herbal paradise. The dream homes we always wanted can be visualized and created in the homes we currently live in.

In fact, as master conductors of our home lives, we can orchestrate our households to flow with sweet melodic beauty. Meals can become dinner extravaganzas. Baking can become French pastry making. Car washing can be transformed into lavish modern water-fountain displays. Even paying the bills can turn into transactions of high finance and abundance. There is no end to what we can create in our minds.

(2) *Work life.* Our jobs are creative outlets; we are paid to use our imaginative thoughts to complete assignments and tasks. Many employers pay us bonuses to bring new ideas to them — these ideas are our imagination in action. Even if we perceive our work to be repetitive or routine, we can use our imagination to create more enjoyable environments.

We can visualize our clients contributing to our endless source of money as they happily purchase all our products or services. We can even envision helping them load boxes of our products into their cars, or we can see them lining up for our services. By focusing imaginatively, our morning coffee break can become an exotic tropical drink that we sip on a sun-drenched beach on an island in the Pacific.

Our problems at work can become opportunities as we exercise our creativity and take the time to create imaginative solutions. We can think our way to better and more delightful careers. We no longer need to manipulate the system to get what we want; we can create positive, effective ways for everyone to gain in the work environment.

(3) *Social life.* Our social time with friends and relatives and our leisure time are opportunities to use our imagination, especially when we get bored and look for something to do. We can create a vast number of options to consider.

We take up hobbies, recreational sports, fitness, and reading because our imaginative thought showed us mental images of what we could do with our time. As long as we have not become static in our creative processes, these activities are recreative. However, if we no longer enjoy doing them, it is time to imagine something new.

That drive to grandma's house can be via the country road instead of the highway next time. Grandma won't mind the little extra missed time; she can take us only for so long, anyway. We can dance the night away without ever leaving our homes. We can play sports instead of watching others play games. We can sit home and draw with crayons to our heart's delight. Our hobbies can become creative outlets to share with others. For many people, hobbies lead to a second source of income and even to a satisfying full-time career.

(4) *Our relationships.* Our involvement with other people offers the greatest challenge and opportunity to constantly use our imagination. Getting the most from our interactions with other people is the greatest accomplishment we can pursue. We can truly push our imagination to new heights by helping others enjoy life with us.

A kiss can become a sweet embrace. A glance can become a hug. The breakfast plate can become transformed into the poetry stand to place our special affirmation cards. The night out can become the night in with our loved ones. The night in can become the night out with our loved ones. Working alone can become playing together. We can watch the rain or look at a sunset together. Making love can become a physical experience that is full of fantasy. The relationship can become the total experience we want it to be — if we use our imagination and our creative process.

SUMMARY

We entered this doorway with the understanding that we have the gift of imagination, that with this gift we allow our Internal Power to be unleashed and we become the creators of our lives. Just as the maestro conducts an orchestra, so can we become the conductors of our orchestras of life. The creative process is ours. All we must do is accept this fact and begin to use the knowledge.

Most of us have suppressed this magical imaginative aspect of ourselves for too long. We must believe in our abilities and in our imagination, and see that this imagination gives us the power to create the lives we wish to have. We may have previously ignored our use of imagination in creating the things we wanted, yet we have always used our imagination, often in a limited way. Now we can take conscious control over our unlimited imagination and learn to work with it at every moment.

> *Imagination gives us the power*
> *to create the lives we wish to have.*

Above all else, we must be willing to experience our imagination. If in our youth we were told not to daydream, we need to make the time now to daydream. When a situation arises that seems to be overwhelming and without a solution, we are presented with an opportunity to use our imaginative thought. *Stop and reflect.* Question the facts. Create a mental image of the best possible scenario and then expand that imaginative thought as far as it will go. When it feels right, make the appropriate choice to bring the best solution into reality. Hold the vision until it becomes physical reality by taking the necessary steps to make it happen. As we gain experience, we will begin to link our successes in physical reality with the original creative and imaginative thought.

When we look at our daily activities, we can recognize the sustained patterns of thoughts that have led us to the reality we experience. If we limit our imagination or choose not to use our total creative processes, we create limitations in our lives and frustrate our creative processes. Each of us has already experienced both sides — success and failure. When we questioned our ability to create something we wanted, we usually didn't receive it. We often failed to take the appropriate steps that would have created what we wanted. Whenever we have firmly held a vision in our minds of something we wanted, we eventually received it. It is absolutely true: If we can dream it, we can create it.

Imagination is our gift. Even the simplest act in life is a result of a thought — and thought has imagination as its foundation. We can now express ourselves through a conscious change in our perspectives of the creative process. Within every imaginative thought is the opportunity to bring something into our physical reality by using our willpower to create it. Be it a meal, a painting, child raising, work, a walk, a new career, a new way of life — everything becomes an imaginative creation if we allow it to be. Our daily structures grow more exciting as we embrace our creativity as a natural fact of life.

PLAYTIME

Project 1

Get some crayons, colored pencils, water colors, construction paper, finger paints — anything you would like to work with — and sit down and draw or paint. If you have not done this for a while, just let your imagination flow. When you are done, sign the piece. Affirm yourself and see only the positive creation that you have before you.

Put your piece up on your wall or refrigerator. Let everyone see it. Accept only the positive comments and let any negative ones float on by. It is your creation, your artistic work.

You can do the same thing playing an instrument, singing, crafts, sewing, or whatever else appeals to you.

Project 2

Take a different route to work. Plan it with a map. Give yourself a scenic drive that goes through or past parks. Give yourself enough time to get to work, but make sure you also give yourself plenty of time to experience the drive.

Project 3

Find new, effective ways to do your job. Approach your boss and get his or her insight. Let people know that you want to be the best at what you do. Make sure, however, that if others don't agree with your new ideas, you respect their way of doing things and cooperate with them. Not every idea has to become a reality for it to be creative.

Doorway Five:
Masculine and Feminine Energies

A VISUALIZATION

We now proceed farther up our hallway, and we are filled with excitement from everything we have discovered about ourselves. Perhaps an affirmation runs through our minds, such as "I believe in myself and my unlimited capabilities." We sprint to the next doorway, seeking what lies within the room. As we face the door, we see that it is split in the center and is made up of two half-doors.

Although we are a bit puzzled, it becomes clearer when we see that the word *Masculine* is on the left half of the door and *Feminine* is on the right. We quickly grab our Golden Key, open both doors, and step into the room.

In the middle of this brightly lit room, we see three stone pedestals standing quite close together. On the two outer pedestals are beautiful marble statues facing each other. One is a male figure, the other a female figure. Each statue is graceful; each figure seems to be full of energy. We intuitively move to the center pedestal, intrigued that there is nothing on it. Then it dawns on us: this pedestal is for us. We step up and stand upon it.

As we stand between the statues, we feel calm, even serene, and we naturally reach out our hands and touch each statue simultaneously. At that moment they become real and lean over to embrace us. We experience equal amounts of masculine and feminine energies harmonizing within us. We feel balanced and complete, and recognize that this is different from being man or woman — this is much, much more. A sense of oneness comes over us as we feel the powerful embrace of being in unity with our two halves. The unity of these energies is yet another important aspect of our Internal Power: the balancing energy within us.

MASCULINE AND FEMININE ENERGIES

Each human being has unlimited potential in life. Our ability to conceive and to fully manifest our reality comes from the true balancing of our innate masculine energy and feminine energy. It is the combined power of the two energy forces that brings us unlimited potential. When we accept and engage these potent sources of opportunity, we embrace the fullness of ourselves and experience life fully. When we understand and use these wondrous energies, we experience our Internal Power.

These concepts may seem strange at first. What are masculine and feminine energies — or characteristics — and how do they help us transform our lives? How do they differ from the traditional understanding of being male or female?

Throughout this book we have discussed how our thoughts have energy. Our thoughts provide the energies of desire and action. These energies motivate us to think, to do, to create. They can also be energies that stifle us, depending on what kinds of thoughts we have.

What are we trying to comprehend when we speak of masculine and feminine energies? What this doorway introduces to us is the concept that masculine and feminine thought energies are parts of each of us, regardless of our gender. They are energies or characteristics because of the innate power they give us to conceive what we desire and to act upon our thoughts.

The concept of masculine and feminine energies is not new. Carl Jung described the male energy as *animus* and the female energy as *anima*. These innate parts of us govern how we operate and interact in our lives. To the degree we exhibit one over the other determines, in large part, what occurs in our lives. The key is to accept both parts equally, regardless of our sex, and balance the energies for the greatest Internal Power.

Male and Female Traits vs.
Masculine and Feminine Energies

We have all been taught appropriate behavior as men or women, depending on which gender we are. Yet many of us never stopped to question who we really are internally. We accepted the roles presented to us and played them out diligently, often without a second thought.

It is generally accepted in many cultures that to be a man is to exhibit only male traits, and to be a woman is to exhibit female traits. Traits, in this sense, are the scripted roles or criteria that our families and our societies dictate as appropriate and that we often accept when we are young. As adults, we continue to play the roles, and thereby perpetuate the cycle. These traits are neither good nor bad; they are simply concepts of how men and women are "supposed" to act in our society. They are external expressions of maleness and femaleness as prescribed by others.

These external characteristics may include how we dress, the way we move and gesture, the work we do, what we do for pleasure, the cars we drive, the sports we participate in, and the books and magazines we read. They may also include who can (or should) cry, who can't cry, who is the head of the household, who leads, who follows, and who runs our country. These traits or roles, however, are not necessarily adequate reflections of what is really going on inside each individual. They do nothing more than describe the outward actions of a person and not the thinking process within.

If traits are defined as external roles that we have apparently accepted, then what are masculine and feminine energies?

If they do not represent being man or woman, then what do they represent and how can we incorporate them more fully into our lives?

Let's consider some typical masculine characteristics or energies (notice that they have nothing to do with male gender or machismo): willpower, analytical thinking, protectiveness, linear reasoning, rational thinking, objectivity, directedness, intellectual, spontaneous, and focused. These attributes tend to come from the left brain. Our physical reality is a result of focused masculine energies, which provide the physical action or power of the will to manifest.

Feminine energy characteristics include imagination, creativity, nonlinear thinking, feeling, holistic insight, intuition, gathering, giving and receiving, subjectivity, simultaneity, nurturing and being nurtured, and balance. These aspects generally come from the right brain. Whether we are male or female, it is valuable for us to cultivate each attribute to its greatest potential. When these attributes are understood and are balanced with the masculine energy, we can then experience our unlimited potential.

Several masculine and feminine energies are also representative of male and female traits or roles, although our male-based society has historically regarded many feminine characteristics as weaker than or inferior to many masculine characteristics. Yet, how we have been so easily fooled! Feminine energies are the originating energies, the creative and imaginative energies, and when combined with masculine energies such as willpower and focus become the total indivisible package within each of us that is unlimited in vision and power. We create our physical reality by the balance of both of these energies.

*Masculine and feminine energies already exist
in each of us waiting to be tapped.*

Understanding that we are more than our gender affiliation or the scripted roles we may have accepted allows us to embrace our unlimited potential. Being masculine and feminine is not to be confused with male or female gender. Masculine and feminine energies are thought energies; they already exist in each of us waiting to be tapped. By acknowledging both sets of characteristics, we can balance and harmonize our thoughts and perspectives. This blending of our true selves assists us in experiencing our Internal Power.

The Effects of Masculine and Feminine Energies

We can readily see many kinds of masculine characteristics in our lives, due mostly to the male dominance of many aspects of our society. Much of the massive building and accumulation of personal wealth during the last century is a direct result of highly focused willpower. So is the creation of the world's superpowers. We continue to see great advances in science and technology — look at how computers have changed in the last ten years, for example. All the advances show what focused willpower can create. These are truly masculine energies. Or are they?

Much of our focus is on getting things done. We have been taught over many generations that men exhibit protective, rational, logical, and analytical traits, and that through the use of "focused doing" we can and will create whatever we put our minds to. Yet when we put our minds to it, we are tapping into the feminine thought energy of imagination and creativity. So, to be successful in using masculine energies, we must accept and use the feminine energies as well. And the reverse is also true. The feminine energy cannot manifest until it has combined with the masculine energy.

In our male-dominant culture, masculine energies tend to be exhibited and exemplified to an extreme. It is not that feminine energies have somehow disappeared in the process. Rather, the knowledge and recognition that feminine energies exist simultaneously with masculine energies have been ignored or suppressed.

It is impossible to have one energy without the other. Both must, by design, work together. Extremes cannot work in the long run; they destroy themselves. A loss of Internal Power comes when we use one energy to an extreme without considering the other. Our massive physical and technological growth, for example, has often been at the expense of our natural environment. This destruction, by not acknowledging feminine energies, has caused a contamination of our life-sustaining systems. We have polluted our water and air in an effort to provide vast numbers of square buildings, congested freeways, fast cars, appliances, and gadgets.

The balancing feminine energies, when acknowledged, have the power to build societies that respect the fragile ecosystem of our planet as well as the people on it. As we bring our masculine and feminine energies into harmony within, we will bring our outward lives into harmony, also.

To have true Internal Power is to embrace the fact that we are simultaneously masculine and feminine. We have the ability to imagine and the willpower to carry out that imagination into reality. For many, however, this has been an unconscious thought process.

Let's look again at a list of masculine and feminine qualities:

Masculine (generally left brain)	Feminine (generally right brain)
Willpower	Imagination
Instinct	Intuition
Linear reasoning	Nonlinear reasoning
Analytical	Holistic
Protectiveness	Feeling
Objective	Subjective
Directed	Gathering
Intellectual	Ability
Spontaneous	Balance
Rational	Giving and receiving
Focused	Simultaneous
Dynamically creating	Nurturing and being nurtured

This list is only partial, but it gives a view of the kinds of energies that exist within us. We must take care not to attempt to add traits that have gender affiliation, for that perpetuates the dilemma we have already created. Rather, we need to carefully observe those energies that currently describe ourselves and those that are lacking. When we understand which energies appear to be lacking, we can take the steps to bring them more fully into our lives, thereby creating harmony and balance. This balance manifests our complete Internal Power.

To be fully a man or fully a woman
is to truly embrace the wholeness of both
masculine and feminine energies within us.

To incorporate our Internal Power, we need to look at the interactions of feminine and masculine energies. This does not mean that a man must become effeminate to embrace his feminine energy. Quite the contrary — it is much more masculine to know, and therefore show, the balance of both energies. For a female to acknowledge and use her masculine energies, she need not become aggressive and start wearing men's three-piece suits. The fallacy is in the stereotyping. These are roles that we, as a society or as a culture, created as a way to shift the focus from the true reality: that we all use masculine and feminine energies. We cannot function without using them both.

The key, then, is to note when we do not use the energies in a balanced manner. If we do not embrace the notion that these energies are already within, however, then we try to compensate in our relationships with others.

Compensating in Relationships

We often seek the opposite characteristics of ourselves in the mates we choose. If women feel fully feminine and cannot seem to embrace their masculine sides, they may seek very masculine men to fulfill their missing parts. Likewise, when men feel solely male, they will frequently seek highly feminine women to create their balance. The problem is that they sought an outside remedy for an internal lack. At some point, they will begin to wonder why they are still un-fulfilled and are longing for more. Their longing leads to frus-tration and often to outside relationships. But the longing comes from their unwillingness to accept that they require both masculine and feminine energies within themselves.

Balance and harmony will come in our relationships only when we view one another as partners for learning, growth, and experience, rather than for providing the ener-gies we lack. A male will never be able to provide the mas-culine energy for his mate, just as a female will never be able to provide the feminine energy for her mate. These energies must be experienced within us for us to fully use our Internal Power. When we learn to accept that another person can never provide for us what we are truly seeking internally, we turn our power from the external to the internal. Our mates can then teach us how to balance the energy we are learning to express and how to embrace the qualities we have ne-glected. Our relationships will blossom in untold potential as we work together to bring fullness and balance into each other's lives.

Seeking the balance of our energies is not limited to fo-cusing on ourselves or on our intimate relationships. Our friends, families, co-workers, clubs, associations, and reli-gious and spiritual organizations all portray aspects of mas-culine and feminine energies. We often seek these other peo-ple and groups as a way to fulfill needs that we don't recognize within. A man may be motivated to look to his re-ligious congregation, for example, to provide him with nur-turing from an external source. A woman may choose to re-main heavily bonded with her father as a way to fulfill missing — actually, unrecognized — masculine energies of objective thinking to balance her subjective thoughts. These kinds of interactions occur daily with all of us. We look externally for fulfillment of our intuitive desire for internal balance and peace. But external sources can never give us this peace in a sustaining fashion; and whenever we look to another for what we already have inside, we subject ourselves to the other person's or group's point of view. It may be similar to our view, but it is never exactly our own. Each of us needs to know who we are as individuals; each of us can find fulfillment only by exploring and developing our vast internal resources.

How These Energies Work

Let's look at an example of a man with healthy masculine energies who is out of touch with his feminine side. He readily exhibits willpower, a protective instinct, spontaneity, dynamic creation, focus, and so on, but when he is presented with an opportunity to be nurturing or nurtured — both feminine characteristics — he may resist and miss a grand expression of warmth and compassion. Men have often been taught that to express their feminine energies or qualities is a sign of weakness or a shortcoming. If we hold the belief that we cannot be nurturing or nurtured because of societal or parental teachings, we perpetuate the cycle of not accepting our wholeness, which, in turn, means a great loss of our Internal Power.

Loss of Internal Power also occurs when a woman accepts the beliefs that she has only feminine characteristics of imagination, gathering, intuition, feeling, and the like. If, for example, she uses her imaginative thoughts and yet doesn't embrace her willpower — a masculine energy characteristic — to physically act on those thoughts, she will be stifled, especially if she has been taught that using her willpower is not appropriate. She in effect loses a large part of her Internal Power. Unfortunately, it is often the case that when a woman does exhibit her masculine energy, she is often considered aggressive, or worse.

One of our greatest challenges and opportunities as we develop our Internal Power is to learn to balance our masculine and feminine energies. If you look at the list of these energies, you can determine which ones you don't readily accept and use at the present. If men use masculine energies and ignore their feminine energies, they are out of balance. If women focus on feminine energies and do not acknowledge their masculine energies, they are out of balance. Men and women bring balance and harmony into their lives when both their masculine and feminine energies are used.

There are other extremes in which a man embraces his feminine energies and not his masculine energies. Likewise, a woman may embrace her masculine and not her feminine energies. These out-of-balance conditions often lead to forms of chauvinism, both male and female, and further complicate our understanding — often keeping us from recognizing our full potential.

How We Embrace Masculine and Feminine Energies

How do we create the balance of masculine and feminine energies in our lives? Do we have to give up our male or female traits to embrace this concept? Accepting the awareness that we, as individuals, are a combination of masculine and feminine energies in no way detracts from our lives, but instead enhances our lives immeasurably. When we recognize the missing or lacking characteristics, or energies, we can begin to create harmony and balance within.

We need not give up our learned traits, but we can look at those traits from newer and higher perspectives. We can choose to expand the traits that truly benefit us, and we can also choose to release the learned traits that have limited us in the past. When we retain these traits because of societal or family attachment, we give away our power. These learned traits often provide an illusion of external power; however, this external power ultimately depletes our energy and exhausts our potential. By shifting our perspectives, we can accept the combined masculine and feminine energies that are the true energies of our lives and allow unlimited potential to be our reality.

To embrace and use masculine and feminine energies, go within and listen to your thoughts. When you pay attention to your thoughts, you can determine which thoughts appear to have masculine characteristics and which have feminine characteristics. Focusing on the energy your thoughts have will allow you to discover which kind you use the most and why. You can then focus on the missing energies, the energies you have been neglecting, and create the opportunity to balance your thought energies and your lives.

Look also to your external reality for guidance. Look at your actions and the actions of others to assist you in recognizing the emphasis of your thoughts. Do you tend to exhibit only masculine or only feminine characteristics? Do you allow yourself to experience the other energies? If not, why? Set aside your scripted roles and acknowledge the fullness of your abilities. Embrace and pursue the use of all your energies, masculine and feminine. To do any less is to give away your Internal Power.

You can look at your relationships, families, friends, and co-workers as opportunities to express the full range of your internal characteristics. Others can help you understand your strengths and weaknesses. This is not a difficult process — all you need to do is shift your perspectives. Thinking in unlimited ways allows you to take full advantage of the unlimited potential your masculine and feminine energies provide.

Stop and reflect. Our ability to think consciously and choose our thoughts allows us to be aware of the reality of our combined thought energies. We cannot have masculine energy without feminine energy. The potential energy of each, masculine and feminine, resides within us and is there for us to engage. Whether or not we are conscious of these energies, they do exist. They cannot be separated; we can only choose not to embrace them. The choice is always ours.

SUMMARY

It has become obvious that our culture emphasizes too much masculine energy without regard to the feminine energies that provide a necessary balance. We have concentrated on our willpower and have frequently ignored or suppressed our intuition and compassion. We have built massive physical structures without harmonizing with our innate energies that help us to nurture ourselves and our world. But it cannot continue. Energy always seeks balance.

When we are unwilling to accept both masculine and feminine energies and characteristics as a fundamental part of us, we turn to other people to complete the balance. Turning to our external world for what we already have within is an enormous loss of our Internal Power.

In our relationships, we can look to other people as partners in our process of growth. We can acknowledge these people with a fresh new perspective and drop any expectations we may have for them to provide what we feel is missing in our lives. Instead, we can begin to experience our complete whole self internally. We can then function as true partners and learn from their views and their assistance. Our Internal Power will unfold at an exponential rate as we allow ourselves to understand and experience both our masculine and feminine energies as we relate to others.

Our masculine and feminine energies provide the energy necessary to imagine and manifest our highest potential. Our imagination, coupled with our willpower, gives us the opportunity to fully experience life. As we embrace the balance and experience the energies we may have suppressed, we feel the harmony and Internal Power that come from this awareness. As we grow in both our imagination and willpower, we inevitably share our understanding of these vital energies with others, which assists the world to balance its perspectives.

PLAYTIME

Project 1

Review the list of masculine energy characteristics and feminine energy characteristics. Compare each category. Try to determine which ones are dominant in you. Which energies do you regularly exhibit? Which do you not use enough? Which do you look to your mate or other relationships to provide?

Project 2

Decide on one masculine or feminine characteristic you want to focus on. For example, you know you have imagination. Work on bringing imagination into every part of your life. If you are loaded with imaginative ideas and never seem to physically create any of your ideas, manifest your willpower to bring about an idea. Start with a small idea and continue working with your ideas until you allow bigger ideas to be manifested through your willpower. Do this until you feel an inner balance between your imagination and your ability to manifest through focused willpower. Pick another characteristic and repeat the process until you feel balanced in that area.

Project 3

Take some time to objectively examine the roles your parents have played in their relationship. What roles have they played in your life? What can you learn about your masculine and feminine energies from this experience? How can you bring a greater balance of masculine and feminine energies into your life right now?

Doorway Six:
The Child Within

A VISUALIZATION

Our spirits are high as we approach the next door on our journey. It is brightly colored in playful hues that excite our curiosity. A warm and friendly teddy bear is happily painted in the center of the door. We have the feeling that something wonderful awaits us in this room.

Our Golden Key unlocks the door, and it gently swings open. We are immediately bathed in beautiful pastel light that emanates from everywhere. We absorb this warm and cheerful light throughout our bodies.

As we begin to look around the room, we notice a little child sitting on a beautifully carved, brightly painted rocking horse. We quietly move closer to the child to get a better look. As the child rocks back and forth, the faint sound of a childhood song comes to mind. Then we realize the child is humming a tune.

As we approach, the child turns to us, smiles a huge, warm smile, and extends both arms toward us. We realize that this precious child is our self of many years ago. We immediately scoop up the child and hold it lovingly against our bodies. Tears of joy stream from our eyes as we are reunited with our younger self.

We have found our long-lost companion. A peaceful feeling flows through us as we realize the freedom of being young at heart. Our child within has long been waiting for us to come and bring it home. We are ready.

THE CHILD WITHIN

We start out in this world as pure, faultless, flawless, curious, and loving babies. From the moment of birth, we have unlimited potential to evolve. There is virtually no limit to what we can become — be it scientist, brain surgeon, mother, dad, professor, president, millionaire, florist, mechanic, or anything else. Our childhood environment sets the stage for these outcomes — or does it?

What about murderers, rapists, and thieves? Couldn't we become these, also? Do our childhood environments set the stage for them, as well? No. It depends on the decisions and choices we make throughout our adult lives. We may be born into environments that teach us certain principles and ideas; as individuals, however, we are responsible for the choices we make as we grow up. The choices we make throughout our lives determine whether we become murderers or millionaires, rapists or reporters. Our childhood environments don't create what we become — we do.

Why does one child from a broken family become a highly acclaimed success while another child becomes a drug addict? Why do so many affluent teenagers become bored with life and commit crimes while their poorer counterparts are taking college prep courses? Why does one child stay shy and passive throughout life while a sibling becomes outspoken and assertive? Why do so many teenagers commit suicide? The questions are endless. No broad pattern emerges that gives us satisfactory answers — everything happens because of individual choice, and the choice process begins when we are born.

If we came into this world pure, loving, and innocent, then this must be our natural state. *Everything else is learned from people, experiences, and events throughout our lives.* We accepted the structures in our lives because at the time that is all we could do. Now, we can do more!

On our path to self-discovery, we have a ready and willing companion, our child within. Here is a wealth of thought energy — memories of early years and fantastic impulsive energies that bring delight, curiosity, enthusiasm, and the natural spark of youth to stimulate our lives. This energy is more than just a feeling — we can literally bring the fullness of our child self right into our immediate thoughts.

What, then, is this child within? Why do we want to bring it home? Where do we find it? Is it real or imaginary? How can the child within really help us?

Our Child

To begin the exploration, let's determine what we mean by the child within. Our child within is our youthful self, the energy of childhood. It is a bundle of beliefs, memories, interpretations, and experiences that we have ascribed to and accepted as fact. In other words, *these are our thoughts from childhood.*

We can learn to embrace this child within by giving it a form in our minds. We can go back into our childhoods through our thoughts, find our little self in our memories, and embrace that five-year-old, two-year-old, or eleven-year-old self. The age doesn't matter. We need only affirm that we have our little self within us. Uniting our child and adult selves is the beginning of a permanent and beautiful relationship.

What can the energy of our child within provide? All the curiosity, creativity, wonderment, spontaneity, imagination, and deep love it once had. These thought processes are empowering and are vital in our lives. Our youthful self is a most powerful ally — a wellspring of Internal Power.

Our child within provides spontaneity,
wonderment, and love.

The child within is a magical aspect of our lives, one that reminds us to take life a little less seriously and a lot more joyously. This eager helper wishes only to persuade our adult self to have fun with life and to be spontaneous, to live wholly in the moment. When this beautiful energy is properly aligned, we have a most valuable companion in self-discovery.

Our thoughts have energy; thought energy motivates us and directs us to act in and react to situations in certain ways. When we need to deal with a situation, we tap into all our resources — not only all our adult experiences, but also our childhood memories of experiences and interpretations of those experiences. Think of what this means! It means that, as adults, we can be further empowered by the energy of our younger selves. We can experience the full range of who we are — including the spontaneous, fun-loving, curious aspects of ourselves.

Of course, the full range of our experience also includes embarrassing moments, temper tantrums, carelessness, meanness, and other responses we have expressed in the past, and these sources of childhood thought energy exist within our minds today as adults. What we need to consider is how to bring these thoughts into alignment for our highest good. Internal Power comes from tapping the strength of childhood energy and using it in conjunction with more mature adult wisdom.

We are often driven by our childlike instincts and memories, and we often don't recognize these influences. At times, these childhood thoughts provide pieces of needed insight just at the right moments. However, the same thoughts may cause us to react in a violent manner to a situation that needs a more mature response, based on the wisdom we have gained from more recent experience. Whether the result is positive or negative, we frequently use the perspective and understanding of our younger selves to address an event or problem — and this can be both frustrating and exhilarating. It is empowering when we tap into the proper thoughts that help us come to useful solutions; it is draining when the thoughts take us into emotional areas that cause us to react in a childish manner. We need to learn how to work with childhood thoughts and incorporate their most positive aspects. We can do it only when we acknowledge the pain and fear of our youth, and heal and release that pain and fear.

When we are aligned with our many positive, useful childhood experiences, we empower our adult lives with this unique energy. When our child within presents misunderstood, biased, and adverse messages, however, we can become derailed and immobilized by these feelings. The child within sends us messages begging for attention and love. When we fail to hear these messages, the child within begins to affect our experiences in our adult lives. Without our adult guidance, these childish experiences will have powerful consequences in our lives. The key is to learn how to embrace our child within, provide the needed relationship, and draw upon one of the most powerful energies available to us.

Bringing Home Our Child Within

To understand how we can function in our adult lives complete with our childhood experiences, we'll first learn how to bring our child home. This simple process requires only a few moments of time and is started by creating a safe mental space and visualizing our memories of our younger self, as we did at the opening of this chapter. After the initial embrace, we can then go back as frequently and for as long as we want to be with our little self. This begins the lifelong relationship and companionship with our child within.

All we need is the willingness and desire to embrace the child self, and then we can proceed. If either is lacking, take the time to ask why. For our visualization to be effective, we want to view childhood thought energy as if it were alive and real in the present moment.

Because we are now the caretakers and companions of our child self, it is important that we create a safe place for ourselves and our child. In this way, we can have open dialogue with our child self, without hesitation.

We are the caretakers and
companions of our child self.

We can visualize this place as a room, a meadow, a forest, a mountaintop, or a house — anywhere we feel safe and comfortable and know our child will be happy. We may choose to read the visualization at the beginning of this chapter again. That room, or elements in it, can be part of our safe place if we like.

To do a visualization, take a few uninterrupted minutes in a comfortable place to relax. You may sit up or lie down. Take as long as is necessary to become quiet within. Count from ten to one to allow your thoughts to quiet down. Let any random thoughts pass through. Relax your mind and body; let go.

As you visualize your safe place, put as many props into the scene as you want. When you feel it is fully prepared, go back into your childhood memories and find your child self. This is your opportunity to experience the child within.

As you go within these memories, you see that the child is waiting for you, waiting for the love, compassion, trust, respect, and relationship you have to offer. Embrace the child within; lift it off its feet and give it the biggest hug of love you have ever given. This is your moment and your child's moment. Know and embrace your child self.

When you are ready, show your child within its new home and let it know that you will provide anything it wants to add within this safe space. Let the child self know that you are together for life, that you will provide all the wisdom and knowledge, love and trust, care and compassion the child needs. When you feel you have accomplished what you wanted in this introduction, bring yourself back into a normal waking and conscious state.

You are now the "parent" of your child within. In return, this child self, this bundle of childhood thought energy, will be your greatest ally. This child can help you become the true unlimited individual you are — all with the marvelous power of thought.

After your first encounter with your child within, return as often as you wish to play with, speak to, and enjoy your new companion. Use these meetings, these moments of quiet reflection, as a way to better understand your life and to empower your thoughts.

The Childhood Story

What we learn in our most formative years sets the tone for what the rest of our lives will be like. When, as adults, we connect with our inner child, we embrace a powerful awareness. Our childhood stories are the collection of all our experiences, knowledge, understandings, and perspectives accumulated from birth and carried into adulthood. They are the collections of our thoughts via our memories — our individual stories. No two stories are alike. When we comprehend the impact our childhoods have on our adult lives, we can begin the process of healing, releasing, and embracing the more hurtful aspects of our past. Our child within will be our helper and constant companion through this process.

All our adult lives, our child within has been searching for a trusting, loving, and constant companion, and we alone can provide our child within the relationship it has been looking for. We are the ones who fully understand our child self and the experiences that it has encountered. In many cases, the child within has been stung by teachings from others that didn't work. This child within wants the best teacher it can have, one that will never hurt or abandon it and will always be willing to work with it. As adults, we are the best teachers and protectors our inner child can have.

In the past we frequently, and unknowingly, have become puppets to our child within by taking the child's perspective. Let's say, for example, we are in a dispute with a friend. The moment the dispute becomes an argument, we begin to call on all our thought resources to defend ourselves emotionally. Within these thoughts are memories of similar instances when we were five-year-old children. Immediately, our child within — the childhood memory thought — kicks in and begins to energize us. We spout off some insane comments that literally come from our five-year-old self. The child within seized the situation and took center stage to deal with the dispute, but that five-year-old has only limited wisdom and experience. The perspective is one of a child and not the broader awareness of an adult.

When we have brought our child within home, however, this process has the opposite effect. Rather than having the child within controlling us at inappropriate times, we work in partnership with our child to bring about more balance and wisdom. Working together, we tap the energy source of our childhood and use the positive perspectives to help us. Let's say, for example, that we are working on a creative project with a tight deadline. The more we think about it, the more stressful and stifled we become. But we can stop and take a moment to go to our child within and view the situation from its perspective. When we tap into the child's creative, live-in-the-moment perspective, our ideas will flow in tandem. We'll use that vast imaginative and childlike energy along with our adult perspective, and we'll come up with solutions more quickly and more easily.

As children, we grow mentally and emotionally through experiences and knowledge, learning from mistakes and opportunities. We also take on knowledge from others and seek approval and understanding from them. We prepare for adult life during our early years based on our surroundings and the people we are involved with — our parents, siblings, relatives, friends, peers, teachers, ministers. Each group plays a significant part in what we come to understand as the experience of life. We associate right from wrong, good from bad, happiness from sadness, all by what we experience during childhood. We rely on others to be functionally okay. In fact, we rely on them to be the best, most capable teachers and role models available.

The child learns much about life through the teachings of others. In fact, we may spend much of our adult lives unlearning things from our childhoods, including beliefs, ideas, concepts, and other forms of knowledge that we accepted in our youth as *our* truth. As adults we must also deal with feelings of guilt, blame, shame, fear, insignificance, and anxiety; we may begin to realize that some of these teachings, beliefs, and feelings are not true for us and that certain perspectives may not be accurate. To discover ourselves fully, we have to let go of many old thoughts and beliefs. The road to Internal Power is paved by our beliefs of today — beliefs that will transcend and displace many of our beliefs of yesterday.

Unfortunately, the child within has also been filled with trauma and despair that are due to the influences of others. Whether gained through childhood experiences or childhood teachings, we want to understand those destructive perspectives that affect the wonderful messages of youth. These colored messages are often the ones that cause conflict within our adult selves and leave us powerless.

A Dysfunctional Environment

Many of our early messages came from people who were simply not functionally okay. Those we have looked to as our teachers and models were often *dys*functional, because as they grew up they learned and accepted teachings from others — thoughts passed down through many generations. We are not, of course, talking about the positive thoughts that truly help us function in life. Rather, we want to look at the adverse thought processes that are no longer valid and that limit our understanding and effectiveness in the world.

What does the dysfunctionality of others have to do with our lives? Look at Christopher Columbus, for example. He believed the world was round at a time when the prevailing belief was that the world was flat. Had Columbus not looked beyond this belief, which had been passed on for generations, he may never have sailed to the New World.

How many of us hold on to beliefs "just because"? Although we may not all wish to be a Christopher Columbus by taking life-threatening risks to prove our inner truths, we must distinguish between what we feel is our truth and that which has been passed on to us. This is especially important when such truth may have come from a dysfunctional perspective.

Consider how we use the knowledge and experiences of our childhoods. If we accept and apply the highest, most positive, and useful traits of others in the events we experience, then we empower ourselves. However, if we somehow have taken on the shame, fear, guilt, anger, sorrow, and other such detrimental emotions and made them our own, then we give away our power. As adults, we no longer need to carry this dysfunctional emotional baggage with us if we choose not to. We have freedom to choose our thoughts.

We must also understand this about childhood: As children, we reacted to situations with our limited experience and understanding, and we may have perceived events and issues differently than they were intended to be perceived. For example, as babies we may have cried for attention, but our parents may have given us bottles because they thought we were hungry. We began to associate attention-crying with receiving food. Could it be that this misperception as babies was the beginning of food or alcohol addictions that appeared much later in our lives? Quite possibly. Was the parent to blame? Of course not. We communicated the only way we knew how, and our parents responded the only way they knew how.

Our perspectives during our childhoods have the limitation of youth without the experience and wisdom of adulthood, and the adult has the limited perspective of an adult view without the benefit of the child's understanding — hence, the continuous conflicts that have gone on for centuries between children and adults. This generation gap, as it is commonly called, no longer needs to exist. We can bring our child home and work in partnership. As we comprehend our childhood stories and embrace the child within, we move on with our lives and incorporate this powerful childhood energy every step of the way.

Begin with Understanding

How then do we begin the task of uncovering the functional part of our life? First, we need to be willing to acknowledge that our parents, teachers, friends, and so on, *cannot be blamed* for our lives and for our upbringing. They, too, are products of their past and did the best they knew how, given their circumstances and understanding. We also cannot feel guilty or blame ourselves for what we did in childhood. We had limited perspectives that often lacked the needed experience and wisdom, and we interpreted events with limited wisdom when the intent of others was not fully understood. We must be willing to accept full responsibility for our lives and consciously desire to forgive ourselves, our parents, and others for the parts we all played in the past. *We cannot blame others for our past or feel guilty and blame ourselves.* The Internal Power process is one of acceptance and responsibility, forgiveness and release.

After this inner work has been done and you have let go of blame and guilt from the past, it is now possible to focus on your daily life. *Stop and reflect.* Listen to your thoughts. What are they saying? Which thoughts appear to be mature adult wisdom, and which ones are more spontaneous and childlike? When you recognize the difference, you create the opportunity to work successfully with the child within. Rather than having your child within control your life to gain your attention, you work directly with the child as a loving parent and incorporate the best of both worlds.

We can tap this vibrant
energy source of thought.

Our visualization process helps us understand and heal our childhood stories, as we go through our childhood memories hand-in-hand with our child. We become able to understand the many things the child within has been seeking. We learn how to provide all of that and much more by going within and fulfilling the child's needs for love, acceptance, wisdom, and understanding. This fulfillment is the healing process.

Looking back into our childhoods is perhaps one of the greatest challenges we can undertake. It also has some of the most wonderful permanent benefits. When we are able to experience our childhoods from nonblaming, more loving, and more understanding perspectives and are willing to heal any pain we experience, we can then release ourselves from tremendous bondage and free ourselves to be ourselves, not what others want us to be. It is important to give adverse childhood events and thoughts an adult perspective with current, mature wisdom. In doing so, we can choose to heal ourselves permanently. By fully accepting the child within, we move on to the wonder of life in the moment, rather than struggling with our thoughts of the past.

Understanding that there was a child of great need as it grew up is the cornerstone of looking at the younger self. This child may or may not have had its many needs met, and those that were not met are probably still searching for fulfillment in our adult lives. Now is our golden opportunity to give that child what it needed as it was growing up. The difference is that we will be parents now and give our child within the affirmations it sought. We don't need to look outside for experiences to fill any void within. We have the opportunity to do what teachers, parents, and friends weren't always capable of doing, because they had many needs from their childhoods that were never met.

We can now take care of our little self. We can love, honor, and cherish our little one the way it deserves to be loved and cherished, fulfilling all its needs. Our little self has been crying out all our adult lives — it has cried out by debilitating us or derailing us in attempts to gain our attention or the attention of others. Now that we have united with our child within, we can learn to love and work with our child, forming a loving partnership.

We must consider that in many circumstances the child may have been somewhat traumatized. When we understand this, we must be compassionate toward ourselves and affirm that we are deserving, loving, and capable individuals. We can go back into the memories of our youth and use current-day adult experiences and skills. The child's perspective in a situation, especially in a traumatic experience, can be greatly altered if it receives current-day wisdom. We discover the power of healing through forgiveness and letting go.

A Personal Story

This is an illustration of child spirit, what can go wrong at times, and the resulting thought energy that carries into adult life. Most important, it shows how we can heal the childhood traumas that have occurred. Let me explain how I worked through this situation.

When I was five years old I lived in Georgia. My father was an enlisted man in the military and we were living in a rental house off the base. We did not have much money. By saving and scrimping, my parents had managed to purchase a small above-ground pool for my sister and me. To me, at five years of age, it was huge and represented the ultimate luxury and fantasy. I needed to use a cinder block stood on its end as a stair to get in. Swimming across the center — it was about nine feet in diameter — was an exhausting experience, at least for a five-year-old.

By the end of summer it was time to prepare for the coming of fall and for my sixth birthday, both of which were approaching quickly. My father had drained the pool and was drying the plastic liner over the clothesline. Dad and I were outside, on this Saturday afternoon, doing our summer yard cleanup.

Dad had just started mowing the yard when he turned to me and asked if I would like to try mowing. I was in heaven. He had never let me touch the mower. He was afraid I would hurt myself. Oh, the joy! Oh, the fear! Oh, the joy! He showed me what to do and then watched as I paraded with the mower proudly, cutting the grass as if it were my ultimate calling in life. My father was pleased; he smiled and went inside the house. I felt as if I had become a man. No, I *was* a man — in a boy's body. I wanted to prove to my father how capable I was, and I wanted his approval for a job well done.

Then it happened: I noticed some tall blades of grass near the pool liner, which was draped across the clothesline and was hanging to the ground. In my youthful zeal for perfection, I moved the mower as close as possible to get those few blades trimmed. Oops — too close! The mower had sucked the plastic liner under it and shredded the edge. Someone had failed to tell me about the vacuum principle created in a lawn mower's blade movement.

At that moment, my father came outside and saw what had happened. I was so scared. He was so furious. He took me inside, scolded me, and then paddled me in the bathroom. He assured me that the pool had come at quite an expense — $29.98, to be exact. I had been trying to do my best and win his approval, and yet, by an innocent accident, I instead experienced tremendous shame and humiliation. My father reacted to this situation at a time when my five-year-old's perspective was highly vulnerable. I was forever traumatized.

What had gone wrong? How could this experience have turned out so differently than it was meant to? Just moments earlier I was on the road to manhood. Now I was scared, hurt, and ashamed. I absolutely felt as if the world had come to an end, and I had no idea what to do. But time went on and so did life.

Although I was not aware of it until many years afterward, I had allowed aspects of this traumatic event to continue to affect my life. For many years I had the idea that to do the "perfect job" would lead to punishment. I was not consciously aware of this process, of course. Instead, my child within — the bundle of childhood thought memories — would kick in and derail or stifle my desire to complete an assignment perfectly. I would always stop short of my true potential. This was a form of self-imposed failure I traced back to this long-ago event, along with some other similar but more minor experiences. I had become unwilling to try my best at something because of the fear of failure if I made a mistake and the shame and pain that would come with it.

Twenty-three years later I realized what had happened

on that eventful day and how it had literally changed my life. I had experienced shame, guilt, and embarrassment, not to mention physical and verbal pain, for a truly innocent accident. My intent that day had been to do the best job for Daddy — I wanted to prove to him, and to myself, that I could be trusted with the lawn mower and the mowing. Yet I had been punished for an outcome that had been out of my immediate control. My child had no knowledge or experience to handle the mowing situation or to properly deal with the response from my father after the mishap.

With my growing awareness as I matured, I was able to change my perspective on that childhood event and have, therefore, changed my adult view of failure and perfection. I accomplished this by revisiting the event in my mind — in fact, I went back and relived it.

Using a visualization, I went back to view the entire experience. My adult self observed the events of that day. Without blaming or judging anyone for the acts that occurred, I allowed myself to experience those events just as a bystander. I noted the facts and separated out the emotions, recognizing that both my father and I were doing the best that we knew how. Because I had already brought my child within home, I knew what was necessary to change this situation in a positive, loving manner. My child needed to hear something else, and as his new caretaker and parent I would tell him.

When the moment came for the interaction with my father and the imminent discipline he was about to give, I visualized myself stepping into the picture and told my little five-year-old child exactly what he needed to hear at that moment. I expressed my adult approval and understanding of his desire to do a perfect job and told him that, unfortunately, accidents occur. I also let him know that the pool liner didn't matter, that it would be fixed somehow. What was important was that he had learned from his mistake and that he had tried very hard to do good. I then walked my child out of the bathroom — unspanked — and down the hall, and ended my visualization.

I took control over the situation and gave my child the benefit of *my* adult wisdom and the love and guidance he so desperately needed to feel and hear those many years ago. I know the process of stepping into the event worked, because I began writing this book two days after releasing the traumatic memory. I let go of my belief in failure and embraced my success.

That was a powerful experience for me, and I have used that kind of visualization to heal other traumatic experiences. I don't blame others or myself for the events. In my visualizations, I provide the assurance that my little child needs to hear. He knows that I will always love and care for him for the rest of my life.

My father, by the way, is fully aware of this story, and we have both learned a great deal from it. Neither of us harbors guilt or negative emotions. In fact, my father had not even remembered that event until he heard it at one of my workshops. We both smile now when I recite it. I am much closer to him than I have ever been, and this is due in large part to my healing myself and releasing any judgments that I may have held, knowingly or not. He knows, and I know, that we love each other very much.

SUMMARY

If we allow our imagination to expand, we can go back in time, via our thoughts, and find our child self. When we find and acknowledge this child within, we can incorporate the wonderful thought memory of our younger self into our current adult lives.

This need not be a difficult task. With our willingness and desire to embrace our total self, we can easily incorporate the child within and its valuable perspective. By using visualizations, we go back into our childhoods to uncover the painful events, heal those situations through forgiveness and love, and release the events by embracing a new thought perspective — an adult perspective. We can use the same process to find our happiest childhood moments, incorporate their energies, and bring those joyful thought perspectives into our adult lives.

By accepting this positive and dynamic thought energy, we empower ourselves with vibrant spirits. As adults, we can now use that box of crayons to draw our dream houses, doodle our corporate fiscal plans, or just plain have fun. The child's superb capacity translates youthful energy into simple and elegant results that will be delightful and fulfilling.

While we experience the new energies we can continue to face negative aspects of our childhoods with our child within. As we help heal the traumatic, fearful events that at times hinder us in our adult lives, we will build more trust in our relationship with this wondrous thought energy. Isn't it time we experienced again what it was like to be a child? Let's experience childhood as adults, bringing the best of both worlds into one. The spontaneous, curious, and imaginative child within can be our greatest ally in life. Allowing the child within to become an integral part of our day brings the delight of experiencing life from a child's perspective.

PLAYTIME

Project 1

Using a visualization, go back into your childhood, pick an event of significance, and view the entire situation as it unfolds. Whenever necessary, give your child within the wisdom you now have so that it can effectively change its perspective and overcome any difficulties that occurred back then.

Project 2

As a way to unite your adult and child energies, go to a playground and have fun. Use the swings and slides. Run and jump. Allow your unlimited youthful self to come out and enjoy the moment.

Project 3

Express yourself through an artistic endeavor. Let go of rigid structures and allow your child within to energize you. Draw, sing, dance, play an instrument, paint, color with crayons, or do whatever else comes to mind. Above all, be spontaneous and have fun!

Doorway Seven:
Unconditional Love

A VISUALIZATION

As we move into the hallway, we feel totally exhilarated. It is as if major weights have been lifted from our shoulders, weights we were perhaps not even consciously aware of. It is a freeing experience. We gaze into the hallway and take in its magnificence; we collect our thoughts.

Before us stands a double set of doors, the seventh and final entry on this journey. The doors are superb: beautifully sculpted with graceful gold-leaf designs. They command our attention and appeal to us to enter.

As we approach, the word *love* magically appears over the doors in radiant letters, and the doors gently open. This door needs no key. It is always open and is always willing to be explored.

As the doors open completely, we feel the warmth of golden light pouring forth from every direction, enveloping us in a warm embrace. We glide into this room, stand in the center, shut our eyes, and feel the power of this golden light seep into every cell in our bodies. We feel as if the light has entered every part of us, and we feel that we are a part of the light. We have entered the room of Unconditional Love — *our* Unconditional Love.

As we stand in the light, we open our eyes and begin to see aspects of our past — the people we have known, the many that have helped us and have been there for us. We understand that they have all done their very best.

We look around and see mental pictures of the people currently in our lives. We feel a sense of deep compassion and love for them, and we are grateful for their presence in our lives.

As we continue to experience the room and the light, our thoughts turn to the future. We see our dreams being fulfilled and we catch glimpses of the people we will be involved with. We see that the future will be just as we want it to be, and better than we can imagine.

Finally, we experience ourselves. We see the people that we really are at this moment. Our hearts pour forth as we realize that we can love ourselves right here and right now. We embrace the reality that everything we have just pictured has been perfect and loving. With our newfound perspective on life, we can in fact love ourselves just for who we are and express this love back out to others. We understand the experience of unconditional love as never before. We know that the time has come to reach deep inside and affirm our personal being. We will never experience deep love from the outside until we experience deep love within. *Unconditional love.* We deserve to experience this love. We deserve to experience it here and now. We can put aside the hurt, the pain, the fear. We can let the golden light of pure love, the love for ourselves, sink in. We can experience unconditional love for self right now.

We now understand that the doorways on our journey have led us to our ability to love. With our Golden Key of *willingness,* we have unlocked our hearts.

UNCONDITIONAL LOVE

We are now entering our seventh and final doorway on our journey of personal transformation. The previous six doorways have prepared us for the final concept: unconditional love. This special doorway, in its golden splendor, is the most peaceful and yet the most stimulating of all the doorways we have passed through. This is the capstone of our journey within. The transformation of our Internal Power is realized when all seven doorways become united in one grand hallway, a symbol of our joyous and unlimited inner selves. Unconditional love will allow us to bring this ultimate transformation into reality.

As we journeyed through our hallway, we learned that choice is a freedom we all share. We all can choose the kinds of thoughts we want to have. We also realized that how we communicate these thoughts, to ourselves and to others, truly has impact. The power of our positive thinking strengthens that impact immensely.

We understood that our thoughts are creative and come directly from our imagination. When we balance this creative thought, which is a feminine energy, with our masculine energy of willpower, we bring harmony and power into our lives. As we accept and understand our child within, that beautiful and spontaneous thought energy of our younger self, we allow ourselves to unite our childhood thoughts with our adult self. When we blend all these areas together, we form the bond and grace that, with the energy of unconditional love, becomes a complete source of Internal Power.

The True Meaning of Love

Many of us have thought we understood the meaning of unconditional love, yet perhaps we should again consider what it really means. Is unconditional love a feeling, something like affection or romance? Is it sexual desire? Is it an expression toward another? What does it mean to unconditionally love another? What does it mean to unconditionally love ourselves? Each of these questions describes certain perspectives of love, depending on our current definition. Unconditional love can also be much, much more.

Let's separate the words *unconditional love* and look at them individually. First, what do we mean by the word *love?* Many have defined love as a feeling or emotion within, a physical vibration in our bodies. It may come in the form of a deep sense of surging emotion or may lead us to tears or laughter. Often we define love as a physical response to either external or internal stimuli. For instance, when we look at another person whom we love, we may get a sense of inner happiness that translates into a melting feeling in our bodies.

Love can also be defined in a more superficial way, with a descriptive meaning. We may use the word casually as an expression, without feeling or truly understanding its essence. Examples are, "I love that house" or "I love the work I do." We allow the word to become just a scaled characterization of events in our lives, as if we rate love on a scale that goes from one to ten: from hate on one extreme to love on the other. What we are really saying is that we use the word as a verb to describe something. Let's look now at love as being something more than just an internal feeling or an external description.

If we combine both ideas — love as a feeling within and as a word that describes aspects of our lives — we come closer to the truer meaning. Love, like all our other doorway concepts, is a thought within. The thought of love has an energy to it. The energy comes from the culmination of all our experiences and memories of love. It incorporates many experiences — the affection from a parent when we were babies, the letter from Grandma at age five, our first kiss at age fourteen, our grieving for Grandpa who passed away when we were sixteen, our marriage at age twenty-two, the birth of our babies when we were twenty-five. These physical and emotional experiences provide part of the backdrop of what we know as love. And yet there is more. Because love is a thought and our thoughts have energy, love is also power: Internal Power.

Love is a sense of peace within. Love is joy and happiness deep inside. Love is an expression of kindness and compassion. Love understands. Love comforts, supports, and cares for. Love forgives. Love also honors, respects, and believes. Love is patient. Love does not judge or show hate. Love does not fear or doubt. Love trusts. Love is *not* aggression, spite, or terror. Love is *not* blame or guilt. Love is so much more than just a word. It is *a way of being* — it is a thought.

Now that we have defined some aspects of love, let's look at the other word, *unconditional.* What does it mean to be unconditional? It is to be without condition — without limit. To be unconditional is to be *unlimited.* To be unconditional is to have no strings attached, no expectations, no stipulations.

If we bring our two words together, we may say that unconditional love is *an unlimited way of being.* We are without limit in our thinking and our expression of thought. If we can imagine it, we can build it. Life through love is, therefore, an unlimited experience.

Unconditional love is
an unlimited way of being.

We have sent men to the moon and back, built bridges over massive waters, and found cures for diseases that have plagued humanity for centuries. When love has been the driving energy thought, we have found no limit to what we can do. When fear has been the driving thought, we have created wars, murdered people, and destroyed environments. Fear is limited thinking; love is unlimited thinking. Unconditional love is an unlimited way of being. What does it mean to be an unlimited being, and how does that correspond to love? How does that relate to a practical definition of love, one that can be understood and used?

Unconditional Love: The Personal Journey

Unconditional love is a journey, an attitude toward oneself and life, a lifelong commitment. The commitment is to ourselves. To completely embrace unconditional love and understand it fully, we must experience it personally. Therefore, unconditional love is first experienced as a personal journey. Our external expression of unconditional love can come only from the thoughts we have within. If we have never truly experienced love for ourselves, we cannot fully express love to others.

Unconditional love is more than an emotion. Unconditional love is a sense of peace, tranquility, belief, understanding, wisdom, knowing, compassion, kindness — all felt deep within. This is a personal definition, because unconditional love is each person's experience. Because each of us will have a different experience of true unconditional love, each of us will have a unique understanding. Internal Power comes from recognizing one's unique experience of unconditional love and then sharing that understanding with everyone and everything.

Unconditional love starts with a thought. Your view of life comes from your perspectives, which are learned and experienced through your thoughts and memories. In the other doorways, we discussed how easy it is to accept other people's views of life. Is it possible that a limited view of yourself and a limited view of unconditional love have come partially from accepting other people's definitions and experiences?

Our personal journey to unconditional love is the vital missing piece in our lives. It is the part that we have deep within, yet search for endlessly in our external reality. We think that after we obtain the luxury car, penthouse, top career position, and large bank account we will then experience total peace and harmony. Those who have reached such lofty material heights know that such things don't provide unconditional love. Just as celebrity athletes know, even though the winning point was made or the Olympic medal was won, there is no magical kettle of unconditional love automatically brewing at home. The sustaining power of unconditional love is there only when it is experienced within. Then, when the ball is fumbled and the game is lost, the athlete knows that he or she is not defeated.

Nothing external can give us what we don't have inside. The harder we try to make external things bring us unconditional love, the further away we move from finding it. The penthouse and the gold medal are only the results of what we are doing in life. Unconditional love comes from the process itself, not from the result of the process.

No external search for unconditional love, happiness, and peace within has ever brought us the rewards we seek. External peace and happiness can never come to us if we don't already have them inside. Because our thoughts create our perspectives, we naturally attract experiences, people, and things into our lives that reflect our thoughts. Remember the Choice doorway? Smile and get a smile back, yell and someone yells back. Smiles or yells first were thoughts in our minds — wherever we focus our thoughts, we will create our reality, both internally and externally.

If we have hate, bigotry, sadness, anger, or terror within, then that is what we will likewise give out to others. If we have love, compassion, belief, kindness, and patience within, then we will empower those around us with this energy.

What about the material search? Material things never bring total joy. They may enhance a feeling that we label as love, but it is usually momentary and doesn't express the internal unconditional love we are looking for. When love doesn't exist inside, in fact, external material reality can become a shackle and an obstacle instead of a source of pleasure.

Unconditional love merely requires the commitment to believe in one's self and to affirm that we deserve to experience unconditional love within. When we understand that it all begins with our thoughts, we manifest unlimited energy. All we need to do is to experience our lives with unconditional love.

How can anything so simple have such powerful effects? It is a matter of thought consciousness. When we are unconscious of our habitual thoughts in our daily lives, we let life control us. If we don't believe in ourselves, we take on other people's beliefs. In every case of unconscious thought, we give away our power. We can choose to love unconditionally and, thereby, have the ultimate Internal Power in our thoughts.

Let's look at some concepts that relate directly to the idea of unconditional love. Recognizing the effects of forgiveness, fear, judgment, guilt and worry, relationships, detachment, and even life and death will quickly help us to overcome often debilitating thought processes and move us toward unconditional love.

Forgiveness

Unconditional love means forgiveness — forgiveness toward ourselves and others. A genuine feeling of forgiveness heals lifelong hurt, trauma, and pain. Forgiveness replaces darkness and distress with unconditional love. It gives us peace and serenity. Forgiveness is the *exquisite healer* in each of us. It is a power to heal others, yet it is but a thought.

Forgiveness is the
exquisite healer in each of us.

How can we forgive others? Why would we even want to? If another has hurt us deeply, should we not hold on to that hurt as a way to remember and, thereby, avoid a future hurt? How can we learn from our mistakes if we forgive and let go? If we have never considered forgiving ourselves for events in the past, why should we start now? These are important questions with a simple answer.

If the past is but a thought and the future is but a thought, then the only moment we have to live is *now*. Holding onto pain and hurt keeps that old negative energy alive inside us. If it is within, then that is what we will have to give out — a guarantee for us to repeat events with similar energy. But that is exactly what we were trying to avoid by holding onto the memory!

Allowing yourself to forgive is a wonderful use of your Internal Power. The process can be as simple as you wish to make it. To forgive yourself, someone else, or even a past event, merely *stop and reflect.* Acknowledge any pain or internal suffering surrounding a person or situation, recognize that it is in your past via your thoughts, and accept that it is within you. When you decide to release this limiting view, you accept forgiveness and allow unconditional love to flow within. No situation in life is beyond an act of forgiveness. This is how to grow and learn from your experiences, and learn to live in the moment.

By forgiving, we release the energies of the past and move on with our lives. The power of forgiveness does not change the reality we experienced in the past. However, it will alter our thought experience of the memory and, therefore, the energy it supplies. Because the past is but a thought, it is only our perspective of a person or an event that we could ever change.

Forgiveness is the healer, through an act of unconditional love. It is a power beyond words, a release, and an energizer. It is not an excuse, a shirking of responsibility, or a deliberate shifting of blame. Forgiveness allows the past to become a great teacher for us in an understanding way. Unconditional love is a compassionate view toward ourselves that allows judgments to dissolve and disappear. In their place, we will have peaceful memories of unconditional love and kindness, of lessons learned, of experiences mastered, and of a journey of life filled with opportunities to love unconditionally.

Fear

Unconditional love does not fear. So why do we give in to fear so often? What exactly is fear? Fear, like love, is but a thought. It is a notion of self-doubt that seizes and controls us every time we allow it in. Self-doubt is really a lack of self-love and belief in ourselves. To overcome self-doubt, we must learn to love ourselves unconditionally.

Fear energy may come from mistakes we made, or it may come from our lack of wisdom and appropriate perspectives when we encountered situations earlier in our lives. Fear may also come from beliefs we accepted earlier in our lives from sources such as parents, friends, or society in general. Regardless of its origin, fear is never a true source of Internal Power. Rather, it disguises the facts and keeps us mired in the anxiety and powerless feeling of the moment. Being fear-based is like being in the dark. Being unconditionally love-based means knowing and believing in ourselves.

Let's look at a simple example. It is Friday morning and we receive a memo from our boss informing us he would like to see us at 4:45 p.m. this afternoon. Our thoughts go crazy. Why does he want a meeting? Why on Friday just before quitting time? Our fearful thoughts begin to race. We recall all the layoffs made in the past. We wonder if we will be fired. We begin to question ourselves for all the times we put in only a one-hundred-percent effort instead of one-hundred-and-ten. We are not able to do a thing all day, because the fearful thoughts have taken control. By the time 4:45 comes we are a nervous wreck. We enter the boss's office. We find out that he just wanted to congratulate us for our recent work on a project, that he is headed out of town and wanted to tell us before he left. Instant relief comes over us. All day was spent in fear for no reason. We succumbed to wave after wave of fearful thoughts; we missed an opportunity to love ourselves unconditionally and to enjoy the moments of the day in peace and happiness.

Where did these fearful thoughts come from? Fearful thoughts, such as the ones in the example above, come from several sources. Teachers may have sent us to the principal when we were in school. Friends may have recently been laid off and have described their fears to us. Daddy may have punished us for something when we were younger, or we may just be afraid of authority figures because of our low self-esteem. Our fearful thoughts come from combinations of experiences and limited perspectives from our past.

Had we stopped and reflected the moment we received the memo, we could have acknowledged the fears and addressed them. Remembering that we have always overcome the obstacles in our lives, we could have replaced those fearful thoughts with thoughts of unconditional love. We could have recognized that we had no control over the situation, until 4:45, anyway. We also could have affirmed our abilities and then imagined the worst-case scenario, the best-case scenario, and all scenarios in between. Then through release, forgiveness, and total unconditional love, we could have gotten back to work and waited to deal with the meeting until 4:45. We would know that regardless of what transpired we

would grow and learn from the meeting through unconditional love.

When you operate from unconditional love and live in
the moment, there is no room for fear or doubt to remain.
Knowing that you have everything you need right now to
overcome any obstacle gives you the courage and strength to
conquer your fearful thoughts. You have always overcome
impediments. You would not be here reading this book if
you had somehow failed to overcome an obstacle.

Love dissolves fear.

Unconditional love for yourself and for others provides
the strength and energy necessary to reduce fear to what it is
— a thought hiding in a dark crevice searching for the light
of day, searching for unconditional love. Loving thoughts
conquer thoughts of fear.

How do you really conquer fearful thoughts? When you
are cast into a situation and find fear quickly overtaking your
thoughts, *stop and reflect.* Forgive and release those thoughts.
This intervention allows unconditional love to flow, and with
your shift to conscious thought you can assess the facts in the
situation. Visualize your ultimate fears, and look squarely at
the worst-case scenario. By visualizing all the fears, you can
keep the thoughts in perspective and create the options to
ensure a peaceful and satisfying outcome.

Our unconditional love for ourselves reminds us of our
unlimited being, and with this knowing we can face fearful
thoughts and watch them dissolve into nothingness. For at
that moment, those thoughts have served their purpose: They
have shown us that even the worst-case scenario, if we are

based in unconditional love, will be something that can be overcome, for life always goes on. When we visualize the best- and worst-case scenarios in any situation, we can act from a true source of power and imagine our numerous options to remedy it. For every question asked there is always a solution.

As we learn to embrace the energy of unconditional love for ourselves and for others, we pave the way to eliminate all fear in our lives. Our Internal Power is fueled by unconditional love. Because these loving thoughts energize us to get the most out of life, we need not be driven any longer by fear, but we can drive our lives through unconditional love. What a truly exciting prospect. And to think that it all comes from a choice of thought — our choice, our thought!

Judgment

Unconditional love does not judge. Another way to help bring about unconditional love is by dropping all judgment. Every time we judge ourselves or others, we express a less-than-loving regard for life. Every human being experiences what it is like to be human — our physical bodies all function similarly and we all have freedom of thought. From this foundation point, we are all equals here on earth. *The rest is judgment.*

Judgment causes separation. Separation causes fear. Fear diminishes our power. Only love, unconditional love for ourselves and for all others, can restore our Internal Power. Are not all humans unlimited beings? If we all share the common ability to think and the same basic physical experiences of the body, this must certainly be the case. Then what is the advantage in judging another, or in judging ourselves?

Judgment disappears through unconditional love.

Remember when our grandmothers told us, "When you point a finger at someone, there are three pointing back at you." (Try it and see — it is true.) Every time we point fingers and blame others, we judge ourselves threefold times and more. How often have we judged other people, other groups, other nations for what we do ourselves? We express judgment toward others when we have no knowledge or understanding of a situation, and yet society, our parents, our ministers, our leaders, and others have said it was right or wrong. Unconditional love comes from accepting what feels true and knowing that we are the source of our Internal Power.

When we judge ourselves, we bring external events and perspectives within. Because we give out what we have within, if our thoughts inside reflect judgment, then that judgment is what we will express to others. If we feel we are being judged by others — a common feeling for many people — we can look at our thoughts for any judgment we hold.

Whenever we focus on other people in a way that blames and judges them, we cannot focus on our own energy and Internal Power. Therefore, we give away our power in the judging process, and we also attract this energy back to us like a magnet. This becomes a continuous cycle, until we break through with unconditional love.

The remedy is simple: Learn to love ourselves unconditionally. When we love ourselves, we discontinue our judging thoughts. When we stop judging our thoughts, we learn to love all others and begin to see all humans as sharing the experiences of life. When we love humanity unconditionally, we drop judgment altogether.

Judgment is a thought, a perspective held within. These perspectives often come from others, through personal experiences, and through acceptance of societal beliefs. The country we live in, the state and community, the generation and family we were born into, our education, work, and friends all play an enormous part in the source of our judgments. Each judgment is a thought we hold.

Judgment takes away our Internal Power by focusing on an external perspective rather than on an internal knowing. As long as we continue judging ourselves and others, we remain powerless, giving our power away to outside forces. The moment we shift our focus toward our own beliefs, we bring love into our lives and withdraw thoughts of judgment.

The next time you feel you have judged or blamed another, *stop and reflect.* Forgive and let go. Seek your own perspective and move on. As you develop this conscious method of thinking, you increase your Internal Power.

Guilt and Worry

Unconditional love does not include guilt or worry. If we believe in our unlimited abilities and know that we live only in the present moment, then through conscious choice we can change our thoughts at any moment. When we accept past mistakes and judgments, accept the things that we have control over, and begin to release all the things we cannot control, guilt and worry disappear.

Love conquers guilt and worry.

Guilt is an area in which many of us give away our Internal Power and limit ourselves. Through feelings of inadequacy and culpability, we often judge and blame ourselves unnecessarily. Our thoughts and expectations of ourselves and others lead us down a path of guilt and worry.

Through a self-created structure, we consciously or unconsciously design a matrix of our lives. This structure becomes our personal judgment scoreboard. Every time we fail to hit a particular mark, we increase our tally of guilt. The feelings of guilt can become overwhelming at times and diminish our Internal Power. In the process, we have through our thoughts become offender, lawmaker, judge, and jury to ourselves.

Guilt is a major contributor to worry, as are fear and self-judgment. Worry is time and energy spent with matters of the past or future. In either case, we consume the *now* moment with our worries. We stifle our ability to create solutions in the present. We become all-absorbed in our emotional response to situations and events, and give away our power.

When we worry about what we have done or *should* have done in a given situation, we give our power away. When we worry about economic conditions, the health and safety of others, our personal financial position or future, we give our power away to these external events. No solutions can come through when we are consumed by worry.

It is important to understand the difference between worry and concern. Concern is healthy and necessary. It is a thought energy that springs us into action. When we are concerned and recognize our unlimited abilities, we seek answers to questions and solutions to problems. When we worry, however, we siphon off our power. For example, if we are concerned about our future, we will take the necessary steps to ensure our comfort, safety, and well-being. But if we worry about our future, we do not create the future consciously because our energy is focused on worrying. We don't take the necessary steps to create our desired future, and we are pulled down by the energy we spend worrying. This kind of thought energy doesn't create — it merely drains and stifles.

The way to overcome guilt and worry is to *stop and reflect*. View the situation. Separate fact from fiction. Forgive yourself and others. Release the guilt and worry. Know what you have control over and release the rest. Replace those powerless feelings with thoughts of love and understanding. Move on in life joyously.

Relationships

Relationships are our opportunities to explore and experience unconditional love to its highest degree. Although we may engage in some activities with special partners, we have relationships with every person in our lives.

Let's expand our definition of relationships to embrace a bigger picture of life. Our parents, teachers, siblings, children, neighbors, co-workers, friends, ministers, and so on are all partners with us in this journey called life. Each is here to assist us in our understanding and experience of life. Yet, so is the mail carrier, flight attendant, police officer, beggar, thief, florist, cashier, and fellow highway commuter. Do not discount these interactions because of the brief time involved in the interaction. Every encounter with every person is a relationship, if only for a brief moment.

All our friends were strangers at one time. How else could they become our friends? The first encounter led to additional encounters, and eventually we decided to label these strangers as our friends. It was all a thought perspective, wasn't it? Then what keeps us from understanding that everyone we come in contact with is really our friend to begin with? In this way we can bypass the experience of living in a world of strangers and reap the rewards of unlimited friendship! Imagine walking down the street and greeting every person as your friend, feeling their mutual embrace in return. What a difference this perspective would make! We can tap into the infinite richness of relationships if we recognize that everyone is our friend. With this thought, our relationships can be unlimited experiences.

Relationships demand a high level of responsibility. To have satisfying and fulfilling relationships, we must be free to be ourselves and responsible for our interaction with others. Relationships also denote a sense of commitment to one another — and this is where many of us begin to shy away from relationships. We may feel that a friendship can be broken up over the slightest difference of opinion. But, if it is a real relationship, we must accept the other person even with those differences. That sounds difficult to do, but in reality, it is not. When we can accept ourselves just for who we are, we can accept other people just for who they are. We constantly learn and grow from one another through our relationships.

When we can accept ourselves
just for who we are, we can accept other people
just for who they are.

You can quickly bring this concept into your reality by viewing every person you meet as a friend in a relationship. You can *stop and reflect.* As you come into contact with people, pause for a moment and think of what those relationships are teaching you. You can embrace every person as your friend, and because you accept them wholly for who they are, you can let them be themselves. Your Internal Power will come through loud and clear as you reach out to fellow travelers and give them your unconditional love.

Detachment

Unconditional love has a dimension of detachment. Detachment is the ability to enjoy people, places, and things for their experiences and for nothing else. It allows the many wonderful gifts of life to flow freely and lets go of the illusion that we own anything physical in life, be it a person or a material thing. We ultimately own nothing but our thoughts. We are but temporary caretakers of the physical things in our lives, which can be taken away from us in an instant. Unconditional love means knowing this about our lives and making the most of this understanding.

We own nothing in life
but our thoughts.

Detachment from material things and experiences puts us more firmly in a position to enjoy them. Remember when you purchased your first new car and parked it at the far end of the parking lot to avoid door dings? How could you ever fully enjoy the car as long as you feared its demise? What about the lovely plastic seat covers that Dad put on the car to protect the cloth upholstery underneath? Three years later the next owner took off the plastic and enjoyed the brand new seat covers while Dad was busy putting new seat covers on the next car. All the while the car — including the cloth upholstery — was meant for his and your enjoyment.

What about the good dishes your mother so carefully put away each year? We all know the ones, that special set that came out at Christmas and Easter along with the warning of "Be very careful...or else." The other 363 days you used plain plastic ones. Was that living? How many things do you own that you are so attached to you never really enjoy? How many things in your life are really shackles of fear? The reality is that it could all be destroyed in an instant. In fact, many of us have learned detachment through physical loss.

To detach ourselves from material things, people, and experiences, we must take a good look at our attachment to them. We must be willing to ask ourselves why we are attached to them. We must also ask ourselves what would happen if the items were taken from us. Would our lives end at that moment or would we go on? When we have successfully reminded ourselves that all material things are meant for our enjoyment and that they can be taken away at any time, we can begin to let go and enjoy the flow of our material world.

We can practice detachment with the people in our lives as well. To fully use our unconditional love, we must recognize that we cannot own, control, or manipulate another person for our benefit. Each person in our life can be taken away in an instant. We, too, can be taken away in an instant. It is, therefore, up to us to get the most out of every relationship through the use of unconditional love. We must view each experience with other people as an opportunity to experience the most out of life and to leave no relationship in doubt that it was complete and full.

To experience full detachment from material things in life, *stop and reflect.* Let's look at our possessions with new eyes, the eyes of unconditional love. Because we are unlimited beings, we create the material things in our lives, so why not create new things as we go along? This can be done only if we make room for new items by letting go of old ones. We must look at every item in our lives and be willing to release it. We must look at every relationship in our lives as well, and be willing to release the other person.

This does not mean that we must discard every possession and every relationship, but rather we must allow people and things to leave our lives when the time is right. When we release, we allow the opportunity for new things to come into our lives. So if we have been in a relationship that hasn't worked or if we have an heirloom that has been passed down for generations, pass it along. Allow others the opportunity to enjoy the things that were in our lives. Let us allow our relationships to move on to new experiences. When we release our attachment to something or someone, we allow unconditional love to flow. We know that something bigger and better will be coming, if we allow it.

Life and Death

Unconditional love means living life and understanding death, the age-old conflict. One of our greatest fears is fear of death, and many of us spend so much time in fear and worry about death that we never learn to live. Unconditional love is knowing that we are unlimited beings capable of anything we put our minds to. We can fly to the moon, call a friend five thousand miles away, or watch a spectacular sunset. So why do we become preoccupied with thoughts of death when there is so much to live for?

Usually, we view our lives in the limited scope of our physical bodies, and we have been taught that when people die everything about them goes away. Yet their memories, teachings, ingenuity, experiences, and spirit all live on in all of us.

Another fact worth pondering is that science tells us our physical bodies totally renew all our cells within two years. That means our bodies today are completely different from our bodies of two years ago. If so, then are we not already physically dying every moment of every day? Are we not giving new life — giving birth — to new cells every moment of every day? Is it possible, then, that we are really far more than just our physical bodies?

Love gives life.

What has caused us to fear the idea of death? Is it perhaps that we really fear life? Is living life so difficult for many of us that we focus on our impending deaths as a way to avoid living? Do we fear the unknown of life after death? Do we fear losing our physical bodies or the pain associated with death? As with thoughts of guilt and worry, if we remain fear-based we cannot tap into our unlimited potential through unconditional love.

How can we overcome the fear of death? We must *stop and reflect.* Ask ourselves, "What does my death mean to me and why do I fear it?" Many of us have been taught to suppress our fear of death and not talk about it. When we approach our lives with unconditional love, however, not only can we speak of death, but we can overcome our fear of it. It is our choice. We can recognize the fear as a thought, and we can assure ourselves that death is not something to fear, but rather is a natural process of life. When we understand the thoughts we have associated with death, we can get back to living. Our unconditional love for ourselves will truly translate into our unlimited being as we go forth and live life. This is Internal Power.

SUMMARY

Unconditional love is more than a concept, a feeling, or an understanding. *It is a way of being.* It means allowing ourselves to be all that we truly can be, and knowing that we can love ourselves enough to create the lives we dream of. Unconditional love is giving ourselves the very best *Life* we can imagine. With such power, we can easily share our unconditional love with everyone and express it creatively. Our unlimited Internal Power, through unconditional love, provides us with wonderful opportunities to care for others.

When we love ourselves unconditionally, we love others and do the things we love to do. We refuse other people's scripted roles and we discard any perspectives that are not true for us. We begin to write our own script of life, using our dreams, desires, and aspirations. We rise above the need to be right for others and choose to create joyous lives for ourselves. We become the unlimited beings we are.

When we love ourselves unconditionally,
we become the unlimited beings we are.

When we forgive others and forgive ourselves, we engage our unconditional love. We see beyond the form of life and the trivial ego judgments, and we choose to invoke our Internal Power of unconditional love. If we blame others for our lives, we give this marvelous power away. Accepting full responsibility for our lives lets us be the radiant and unlimited people we truly are.

Unconditional love means letting go of fear. It allows the gentle nature of unlimited thinking into our lives and allows us to experience our Internal Power firsthand. We can visualize ourselves on the other side of any problem, and by doing so we experience our unlimited ability to overcome the situations we fear the most. Now — in this moment — we have the opportunity to end our old journeys of fear and embark on our new journeys of love.

Judgment toward ourselves and others will dissolve as our unconditional love grows within. The power that we reflect back into our world will be the Internal Power of unconditional love. This extraordinary power allows us to have a regard for life on every level, as we perceive and understand the magical connection that bonds us to the world we live in. We begin to see past the veil of separation and realize our potential to work as whole, unlimited beings.

We can live our lives joyously, without worry and guilt, experiencing every moment and savoring its exquisite splendor. This is unconditional love in action. We can release our guilt and discontinue our worry. We can experience all of life in this moment, *the now moment.* Living in the moment, we learn to detach from the material things surrounding us — and thereby begin to enjoy them more fully, recognizing that they are here for our pleasure.

Through unconditional love, our relationships unfold into the beautiful experiences they are meant to be. We can begin to share our love with every person we encounter. We will no longer meet strangers; we will begin to greet everyone as a friend. This alone is worth the experience of living!

As we choose to experience the full power of unconditional love, we can let go of our fear of death. The natural process of death does not bring an end to life; instead, it brings birth to a new awareness and experience of life. It reminds us to live completely in the now moment and to never put off living *Life* for tomorrow. As we recognize this unlimited perspective, we can begin to experience life for what it is and what it provides in every moment. When we do this, we truly begin to *live.*

We cannot wait for love to come to us, for it will not. The paradox is that it is already here: It resides within each of us. It always has and it always will. *For love is but a thought, a feeling, a perspective, a way of life. We are love.*

PLAYTIME

Project 1

Look into a mirror and tell yourself, eye to eye:
"I forgive myself."
Then say:
"I forgive others."
Then say:
"I love myself unconditionally."
How does this experience feel?

Project 2

Being able to love ourselves allows us to love others. Take time to tell someone that you love him or her.

When you are in public, look around at other people and see them as your equals. Recognize that they are also human beings who experience life. Begin to look at strangers as your friends. Treat them as if you have always known them and see what happens. Build on this foundation and for one day begin to express unconditional love toward everyone you come in contact with. Do this for one week. For one month. For life.

Project 3

Loving yourself unconditionally means creating experiences you enjoy. Give yourself a well-deserved gift of something you love to do. Take a bath, plant some flowers, go out for dinner, play a sport, take a walk in the woods, read a book. Remember, this is your time for you. Be good to yourself and live in the moment.

A New Beginning

Every moment of every day is a new beginning! We have the immense opportunity to create the lives we wish by allowing ourselves to begin again. This opportunity is available to us at every moment. What a wonderful prospect! We can put aside our limiting beliefs and embrace the knowledge of our unlimited potential right now. We can consciously choose our thoughts and create the reality we seek to experience. It is up to us. It is our choice. It is but a thought!

Let us repeat this powerful statement: *Every moment of every day is a new beginning.* This is the simplest fact of life. Each of us has the ability to start over in life at every moment. Every feeling, emotion, perspective, experience — every thought — automatically dissolves from one instant to the next. True, most of us attempt to recapture some of our thoughts by holding on to them, and when we hold on to our old thoughts, we have no opportunity to allow new thoughts in. We simply stop living when we concentrate on our past. The same can be said about our future: When we look ahead to see where we are going, and stay focused in this perspective, we miss out on the opportunity to see where we are right now. We have also stopped living.

How can this be? If we stop looking backward or forward, how can we tell where we have been or where we are going? But if we miss out on the now moment, we have lost everything to time itself. We have allowed our limiting thoughts to carry us past an opportunity to experience life, because we have kept away from the current moment. By holding on to the past or the future, we relinquish our experience of life right now. By living every moment, we experience a new reality and a new beginning in the physical now. Remember, the current moment is the only moment we can experience in physical reality. Everything else is a thought.

Now is the only
moment we have.

Does this mean we should selfishly run our lives? Absolutely not! Living in the moment means believing and knowing one's self to such a point that the material ego attachments cease to exist. We become detached from the thought that we need to have something, or someone, in our lives solely for the purpose of fulfilling an internal lack. Instead, when we are fulfilled in the moment, we allow all the good in life to flow freely to us and through us as the experience it is meant to be. Living in this way, we become the unlimited beings we are and we live the life that fully expresses our Internal Power.

What about planning ahead or learning from our past? Should we ignore our memories? What about our goals for the future? Memories of the past and thoughts of the future are useful only when we are empowered by them and take action in the present. If we are learning in the now moment from memories of the past, it is uplifting and helpful. However, if we are focusing on our memories and are attempting to relive the past as a way to avoid the now moment, we are giving away our Internal Power to those thoughts. The same can be said for concentrating on a future goal or desire. If it consumes our now moment and leads us to indifference and non-action, it is best to return our thoughts to the current moment and experience our unlimited potential here and now. After all, we can begin to create our future only by the action we take right now.

Why all this focus on the fact that every moment is a new beginning? It is because of the reality that it represents to us: We all have the ability to start over in life at every moment. We can literally chart a new course in life by the thoughts and actions we take when we begin anew. This is especially important to recognize when we have caught ourselves being unconscious and wrapped up in our limiting thoughts. The moment we become consciously aware of what we are doing, or have been doing, we can start again and choose new thoughts and unlimited perspectives.

For example, when you read this book and practice some of the exercises, you may become aware of the thoughts you have, begin working with them, and learn to choose your highest and most unlimited thoughts. Your life flows easily and happily. Then a few days pass and you suddenly realize that you have been depressed or anxious about something. What happened? You have slipped back into an unconscious thought process. You have allowed some external circumstance or a combination of events to trigger your unconscious thoughts, and you have allowed them to take over.

You always have the opportunity to start again. You can choose a new beginning by choosing new thoughts. You do not need to hold on to the depression, anxiety, fear, or whatever that has triggered the shift; you can let those old thoughts go. In their place, you can choose unlimited thoughts and perspectives. You can use this process every time you become conscious of limiting thoughts. The process of starting again will ensure that you are always living every moment of every day as a new beginning.

BEING OURSELVES

If we want to experience life to the fullest, we first have to discover who we are. We need to discern what is important to us in life. We must decide which of our thoughts are reflections of our true inner selves, and which thoughts and perspectives are layers of personality that we use to hide behind. Distinguishing between our limiting thoughts and the unlimited potential that resides within allows us to embrace our Internal Power.

We can better understand who we really are if we are willing to look at our inner selves objectively. Then we can set aside the limiting beliefs and perspectives we may have accepted from others. We can shed the masks, the layers of personality, the illusionary roles we have been playing for others and embrace our true inner selves. We can choose to see our world and reality any way we want. We no longer need to be something for others. We need to be something for ourselves — we need to be us.

It all comes down to a matter of our consciousness. If we wish to be actively involved in our lives in every respect, we need to consciously choose our thoughts and perspectives. Otherwise, we will passively continue to live life from one random thought to the next, like a roller-coaster ride with no end. We need to make the commitment to realize our conscious thought processes. We are the only ones who can make such commitments and be capable of carrying them out. It is our responsibility. It is our choice.

Our roller-coaster ride has frequently been a problematic and unhappy journey, and we have had no apparent control over our destiny. We have created our lives by allowing our unconscious thought processes to run our lives. We have been literally hanging on for "dear life" to the point of becoming merely a part of the mechanized ride itself. We can change all that right now. We can take charge of our lives and transform our roller coaster into a train, becoming grand conductors of our vehicles. In this now moment, we can choose a new beginning.

We can take control of our lives and, therefore, our destinies by becoming our unique unlimited selves. We can release our judgment, fear, anger, guilt, hurt, and pain, and allow ourselves to experience the love, wisdom, peace, compassion, and understanding that Internal Power provides. We will have the lives we seek when we love ourselves unconditionally and are willing to settle for nothing less.

By choosing our thoughts, living in the moment, and finding out about ourselves and our potential, we can become the unlimited people we truly are.

By choosing our thoughts, living in the moment, and finding out about ourselves and our potential as described in the Seven Doorways, we can become the unlimited people we truly are. We can heal ourselves by facing our fears and understanding our power to overcome them. We can share our thoughts by communicating effectively to our world. We can choose to learn from everything and from every situation, and accept the very best life has to offer. We can become the creative people we really are. We have the power within to gather the resources we need and put these resources to work for us. Our childlike spirits can guide us to become spontaneous and excited in the now moment. Finally, and most important, we can love ourselves unconditionally.

Knowing Ourselves

To be ourselves, we have to know ourselves. The Seven Doorways have opened us up to new understanding and ideas that shed light on our current thoughts and perspectives. Each doorway provides the opportunity to go deeper into the source of our thoughts to help us better know who we are. The doorways also provide us with the necessary awareness to work directly with the unlimited potential of our thoughts.

We understand that every thought we have has an energy to it. We are also beginning to see the importance of the thoughts we have and our conscious involvement with them. Our thought energies provide us with the means to act upon our lives. We make the choice through the kinds of thoughts and perspectives we have. We can either affect our reality through conscious choice of thought or have our reality created for us through our unconscious thought. We control this gateway to our unlimited potential; we undertake the self-discovery process ourselves.

We are the only ones that truly know ourselves and can work with our thoughts. The choices we make determine our lives and the perspectives we hold. We are the only ones who can make a difference in our lives.

Do we have to become superhuman to live in the moment? Do we have to fear the choices we must make? We have only to be willing to love ourselves and believe in ourselves enough to become all that we really are — and we have to be willing to take risks, which really consists of allowing ourselves to live in the moment, happily and joyously.

We are never alone on this journey. There are many people who have a wealth of experience and knowledge who can assist us; we need only ask and be open to receiving. We can absorb the best everywhere. We can learn through many ways. By watching others in action, like our friends, co-workers, and children, we can begin to accept the highest and best aspects of others. We can find positive life experiences and help in everything we do and everyone we come in contact with.

When problems or difficult situations arise, we can acknowledge them, seek positive perspectives, and release negative thoughts. We can deal with any event one step at a time, one moment at a time. When we embrace our Internal Power, we know that we proceed to the other side of any situation, fully experiencing the lessons and wisdom that the problems provide. We can take on obstacles and challenges with delight. This is our opportunity to shine within, to discover our power, to come out stronger, and to succeed.

Internal Power is knowing that we can tap into every resource available to us, including ourselves. We take the parts that work for us and discard the rest. We determine what is right for us, and we are willing to risk and to grow. We accept our mistakes, learn from them, and move on, discovering in the process that we can laugh at ourselves and enjoy every moment we have. Knowing and believing in ourselves and our unlimited potential is knowing peace and joy!

Honoring Ourselves

Honoring ourselves is allowing our thoughts to be peaceful and unlimited. It is focusing our thoughts on the reality we are choosing to create. If we are peaceful within our thoughts, then we are honoring our lives. If our thoughts are in conflict with our outer reality, it is an indication that we are not honoring ourselves.

We honor ourselves by focusing on our highest and most unlimited and loving thoughts. When we are balanced within, we can communicate and share those thoughts effectively to our external world. This may be viewed as an act of selfishness, yet it is selfish only in the sense that we are choosing to focus on our thoughts and inner guidance to conclude what is right for us. If we are truly acting out of love, whether for self or for others, it is not selfish — rather, we are being selfless.

We honor ourselves and others by cultivating the unique potential in every person and recognizing that we need not be dependent on anyone for our well-being. We must also ensure that no one becomes solely dependent on us. We can share in our relationships. The Internal Power process recognizes the unlimited potential in each of us and ensures that no external control is operating. All of those around us, including our children, will grow with greater confidence if we share the vision of their unique and unlimited potential.

When we honor ourselves,
we honor others.

A major shift of awareness comes in understanding that we are not responsible for other people and their problems. We cannot change other people; it is impossible. We can only change ourselves and, by doing so, we can help other people to grow and change. Likewise, we no longer need to allow other people to have control over us. We can let go of other people's criticisms, comments, expectations, and disappointments. We can always learn from others, and we can gratefully accept their assistance when offered, if we wish to do so.

Helping Ourselves

The way to Internal Power is paved by our efforts. We help ourselves by using all our resources, awareness, and understanding. We allow ourselves to take risks to ensure our personal growth and happiness, and we learn and grow from everyone around us. We live in the now moment, honoring our thoughts. We energize our lives through our unlimited thinking.

We begin this process by learning to *stop and reflect.* What does this mean? To stop and reflect is to pause in our thoughts when our "mental flag" goes up. This flag is the part of our process of mental awareness that notifies us we must pause and acknowledge our thoughts. It is easily done and is learned through practice and experience.

When we begin to listen to our thoughts and to focus on the energy they provide, we can consciously begin to create a new reality. We can begin to visualize the kind of life we want to have, and we can start taking the steps necessary to bring this life into physical reality. Our Internal Power is built by taking one moment at a time. Because we know that we have the unlimited potential to obtain all that we desire for peace and happiness, we know that every step we take will get us where we want to go.

Is it realistic to believe that we can have the life of our dreams? With all the apparent pain and struggle in life, how can we ever be happy? There are as many situations as there are people in the world. We can let go of the excuses we have that have limited us in any way in the past. Knowing our unlimited potential means we can take the responsibility to discover ourselves and become unlimited in thought and deed.

When we help ourselves, we help the world around us. When we grow, the world around us grows. When we love, the world loves us. The reverse is also true. When we hate or manipulate our world and the people in it, we experience hate and manipulation in return.

THE JOURNEY CONTINUES

As we close this chapter, we close a mini-chapter of our lives. Hopefully, we have learned a great deal about who we are and the unlimited potential that we have within. We have absorbed a lot of new perspectives and have allowed our minds to expand in many ways. We have experienced many new facets of understanding and have persevered to the other side of many of our perceptions, limiting beliefs, and thoughts.

We began this journey by entering a doorway called Choice. There we found how we create our own reality by the thoughts and perspectives we choose from within. We progressed through the Seven Doorways using this fundamental understanding of choice. Our final doorway brought us to Unconditional Love. This unlimited potential to love and believe in ourselves and the world around us has brought us to the pinnacle of our journeys.

There is one more step we must take to realize the total Internal Power transformation: For the Internal Power process to be complete, we need to weave unconditional love into the very foundation of every choice we make. We can transform our lives by allowing unconditional love to guide us in our Communication, in our embrace of the Child Within, to help us experience our Masculine and Feminine Energies, our Creativity, and our Positive Thinking. The blending of Choice with Unconditional Love is our Internal Power in action.

It is time for us to incorporate all the parts that work for us in becoming our unlimited selves. We can share our newfound wisdom by expressing ourselves to the people around us. We can experience the richness of life by living it.

When you are willing to expand your imagination, you truly live in a limitless world. There is no limit to what you can dream of or create in your life. *When unconditional love guides the way, all things are possible.* Allow yourself to dream and hold visions deep inside of the world you truly want. As you hold those visions, you will create the reality you seek.

Life is a grand and glorious experience; all you need to do is live it, opening your eyes to the world around you and seeing it for what it is. View the world with enthusiasm, pleasure, optimism, and yes, lots of laughter. When you enjoy the world, it will enjoy you! You are now ready to choose your next adventure on your life journey. What will it be? It is entirely up to you. It is your choice. It begins with a thought!

The journey continues....

Epilogue

I have traveled to many places and met many people throughout my life, and one point has become obvious to me: *We are all one humanity experiencing life on earth.* In many ways I feel that I know you and that you are my friend. Even though we may never meet physically, I extend to you my friendship and unconditional love. I have thoroughly enjoyed this opportunity to write to you about my beliefs and understanding of life. I hope that in some way I have assisted in making your journey a little easier and more enjoyable.

Writing this book has been an expression and communication of thought. It embodies the self-discovery process. I believed in myself enough to choose to create this material, and I believe in your unlimited potential to pull together all the resources you need to create the life you desire. I know that you can choose the appropriate people, books, tapes, situations, relationships, events, experiences, and whatever else you may need that will help you continue on your own path of self-discovery.

Your personal potential is unlimited. Use your imagination and create the life you dream of! Be spontaneous and curious; pay attention to your thoughts and work with them. Gather your resources and manifest your reality; share your loving thoughts with everyone, and listen to others. Think positively every step of the way. Through it all let your heart guide the way.

Love, light, and peace,
Harold Becker, 1993

For information about Harold Becker's seminars, contact New World Library.

New World Library is dedicated to publishing books and cassettes that help improve the quality of our lives. If you enjoyed *Internal Power*, we highly recommend the following books from New World Library:

Creating Affluence by Deepak Chopra, M.D. The world-renowned healer presents a step-by-step plan for creating affluence and fulfillment on all levels of our lives.

As You Think by James Allen. An updated and revised edition of *As a Man Thinketh*, this classic has inspired readers for nearly a century. (Also available on cassette.)

Creative Visualization by Shakti Gawain. This international best-seller (over two million copies in print) gives us easy and effective ways to use our imagination to create the life we want.

The Perfect Life by Marc Allen. This powerful book shows you step by step how to map a course that moves you toward the realization of your dreams.

For a complete catalog of our fine books and cassettes, contact:

New World Library
58 Paul Drive
San Rafael, CA 94903
Phone: (415) 472-2100
Fax: (415) 472-6131

Or call toll free:
(800) 227-3900; in California (800) 632-2122